Foreword

Headline Stories

Family Stories

Fans' Stories

Moving Stories

The Business Story

21st Century Stories

The Numbers Game

TOP OF THE LEAGUE!
WF1
WF2
WALKER FARRIMOND
MITSUBISHI
LOMESHAYE MOTOR PARK, NELSON,
LANCASHIRE. BB9 7DR
TELEPHONE: 01282 602602
MITSUBISHI
MOTORS
RE-INVENTING THE WHEEL
Walker
Farrimond
VOLVO
WALKER FARRIMOND
ACCRINGTON
Sydney Street, Off Burnley Road,
Accrington, Lancashire BB5 6EG
Tel: 01254 392222

Foreword

Jack Walker

Blackburn Rovers has played a major part in my life for as long as I can remember.

Like so many others who will read with keen interest the pages of this book, I live and breathe the club.

That is simply because, first and foremost, I am a Rovers' fanatic.

Nothing gives me greater pleasure than to see us win and nothing causes me more despair than when we lose.

My Ewood Park years have included plenty of both; I have seen good times and bad, promotions and relegations, cup triumphs and cup disasters, memorable victories and lamentable defeats, although the highlight has got to be our glorious Premiership success of 1995.

But through all the thick and thin, one aspect has remained constant, my unswerving faith and belief in the club itself.

To be involved as a fan has always been a privilege. To be involved as a benefactor has always been an honour.

Like all of you I get a fantastic buzz out of just being present at the games. Even now, so many hundreds of matches down the line, I still feel the adrenaline pumping through my veins in the lead up to kick-off time.

It is a truly marvellous feeling when people come together as one, united in their total love and support of a team and a club.

Whatever other roles I may play, it is very gratifying for me to know that come 3pm on a Saturday afternoon I am just another ordinary supporter ready to cheer on the Rovers.

That is why my goal has always been to give this club the means to compete at the highest level. I know just how much every fan who pays hard-earned cash at the turnstiles pines for success.

We all want the same thing; not that you can win all of the time, as the thoughts and recollections of the people of the club in the chapters of this book will testify.

These pages will themselves go down in history - a celebration of 125 years of a wonderful football club, my football club and your football club.

We are all the heart and soul of Blackburn Rovers and, in thanking you again for your support, can I toast a marvellous achievement and raise a glass to the next 125 years.

Headline Stories

Headline Stories

1911-12 – First Division Champions

The early Rovers were in real danger of being labelled a "cup team"... no fewer than five glorious FA Cup triumphs before the turn of the 20th Century.

But could they repeat such success in the cut and thrust of league action? Clearly not, for in the first 30-odd years the best they managed was to finish third, in both 1890 and 1910.

All that was about to change in the 1911-12 campaign when Rovers, under the careful guidance of Lawrence Cotton, strode proudly to a first ever League Championship.

The season started with a win over Bury thanks to a double strike from Walter Aitkenhead, but three games without a win left Rovers fans thinking more about the issue of relegation.

However, a crucial win at White Hart Lane, where Tottenham were beaten 2-0, put Rovers back on track.

A draw against Manchester United followed, before wins over Liverpool and Aston Villa saw Rovers climbing the table. A 4-2 defeat at Newcastle was not enough to dampen the spirits of the Rovers players, Aitkenhead in particular, who had already bagged six goals.

Sheffield United, Oldham and Bolton were all beaten before another setback at Bradford brought only Rovers third defeat of the season. Woolwich Arsenal were thumped 4-0 before Manchester City took both points from Rovers' trip to Maine Road at the start of a difficult December.

Everton were beaten, but a run of four games without a win seemed to have put paid to Rovers' title ambitions. Finally, Rovers won at Bury with goals from John Orr and Joe Clennell to round off a satisfactory but unspectacular 1911.

Above Right:
The F.A. English Cup

Far Right:
Members of the Championship Squad

On New Year's Day local rivals Preston were beaten 3-0 in the second of a four game winning streak that propelled Rovers back up the league once again. In fact, Rovers went unbeaten for eleven games, a run in which Aitkenhead and George Chapman proved a lethal partnership.

Rovers were scoring goals from all areas of the pitch, with Orr chipping in with several spectacular strikes, but they drew a blank against Bolton as the Wanderers ended their unbeaten run. However, the team then went on another run of five games without defeat to give themselves a real chance of championship glory.

Having been knocked out of the FA Cup at the Semi Final stage by West Brom, Rovers were now focusing all their efforts on the league. However, title ambitions took a massive blow when Arsenal took revenge for the defeat earlier in the season with a 5-1 drubbing. To make things worse, Rovers couldn't even score themselves, an own goal from Ducat preventing the Gunners from becoming only the ninth side to keep a clean sheet against Cotton's side all season.

Fortunately, three points from Rovers last three games, which included a last-day defeat at Manchester United, was enough to hand Rovers the title. No longer were they concentrating only on the cups.....

1. What is Richard Birtwistle's main claim to fame

(He scored Rovers first goal)

2. Which local club, now more famous for Lancashire League cricket, provided the opposition for Rovers first-ever game?

(Church)

3 Which club, also relegated from the Premiership in 1999, beat Rovers 6-0 to knock them out of the FA Cup in the first year they entered the competition?

(Nottingham Forest)

Headline Stories

1913-14 – Champions Again!

Above: Pictured with their Football League trophy from the 1913-1914 Season are Blackburn Rovers' championship winning side

Above Right: Pre 1940 footballs were always tan-coloured and not waterproof. The lace was present because there was no technique for stitching the final panel

It is always the same, you wait thirty-odd years for a championship then two come along at once – well nearly!

Having failed to repeat their title success of 1911-12 (they actually finished fifth in 1912-13), Rovers' main worry at the start of the 1913-14 season was the lack of cover up front.

Walter Aitkenhead had finished the previous season with 12 goals, but it was inside forward Eddie Latheron who emerged top scorer with 14. George Chapman had lead the attack throughout but had only managed nine.

However, the directors decided to stick with the trio and the gamble seemed to have paid off as Rovers ended up winning their first five matches, scoring 20 goals in the process. Chapman notched six of them and Latheron chipped in with three as Aitkenhead watched from the bench.

It was Chapman again who scored the goal that saved Rovers their first defeat of the season as Sheffield United held the side to a 1-1 draw. In fact, it was not until November 1st that Rovers were defeated, a narrow 2-1 reversal at Sunderland ending an unbeaten streak in the league stretching back 17 games to March.

Rovers bounced back to thrash Everton 6-0 before dropping another two points at Bolton. Chelsea were then beaten before the visit of Manchester United to Ewood Park signalling only the second home league defeat in a year.

Undeterred, Rovers continued to brush the opposition aside. Three games in as many days brought thirteen goals as Rovers beat Preston twice (10-1) on aggregate over Christmas!) and drew with Liverpool.

However, as the New Year dawned, the team failed to win for four games, a run which included a 3-0 defeat at Middlesbrough.

The directors realised that it would be necessary to bring in another forward to bolster the attack. Before long, the hunt was on.

Meanwhile, the team's fortunes had taken a turn for the better. Aitkenhead had been restored to the side following Chapman's loss of form and the striker was beginning to reward the faith shown in him.

Two in two games against Derby and Manchester City gave him a good chance of retaining his place, until the club paid a record fee of £2,500 for Percy Dawson.

Dawson soon shifted Aitkenhead, who would play no further part in the campaign other than a handful of appearances at centre half. The new man scored his first goal for the club in a 2-0 win over West Bromwich Albion.

A further two wins and a defeat followed, before a 0-0 draw with Newcastle handed Rovers their second title in three seasons. Rovers didn't stop there, however. The title hangover saw Chelsea claim the points at Stamford Bridge, but Rovers gave the Ewood crowd the perfect thank you with a win over Oldham before finishing off the season with a 0-0 draw at Manchester United.

The following season proved something of a disaster. The outbreak of war brought about the tragic death of Latheron and mid-season injuries to Dawson and Danny Shea put paid to further title ambitions.

Despite such setbacks, Rovers finished in a commendable third position, but the club then had to wait 81 years for another championship win.

4 In which year did Rovers first reach the FA Cup final?

(1882)

5 Which "other cup" did Rovers win in 1882?

(The Lancashire Cup)

6 When Rovers were relegated in 1898, which club saved their top flight status by suggesting that the league be increased to 18 clubs - Preston, Burnley or Blackpool?

(Burnley)

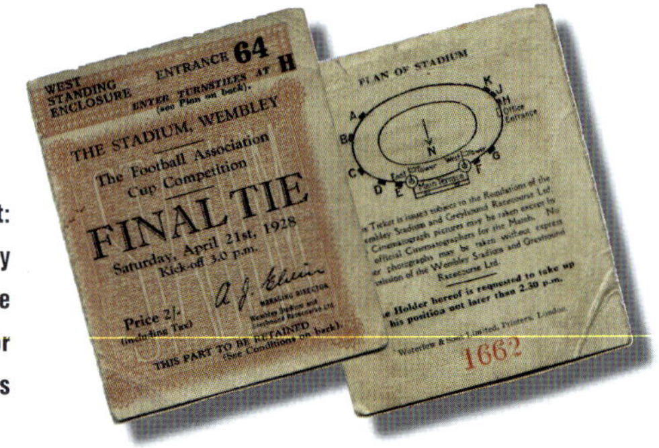

Right:
1960 Wembley Stadium Cup Final Tie Ticket stubs for Blackburn v Wolves

Headline Stories

1927-28 - FA Cup Winners

Below:
1928 Cup Final Programme from Blackburn Rovers -v- Huddersfield

Bottom Right:
Newspaper cartoon from the front page of The Sports Telegraph dated Saturday April 21st 1928

A mediocre league campaign is usually the cue for managers to start spouting phrases like "re-building period" and "rub of the green", but Rovers legend Bob Crompton preferred actions to words. So he brought home the FA Cup.

Rovers had already lifted the famous trophy five times by the time the third round presented them with a home tie against Newcastle United. The first half of the season had not been a disaster, but after just eight wins, few people were forecasting silverware for the Ewood Park trophy cabinet when they gathered at their New Year's Eve parties.

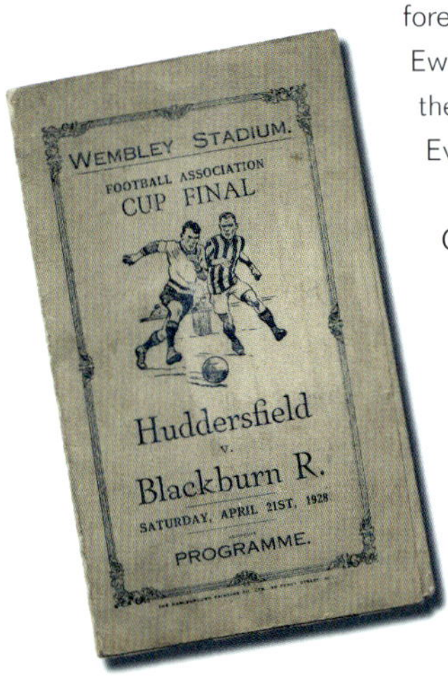

Crompton, still in his position as honorary team manager, had already lost prolific striker Ted Harper to Sheffield Wednesday. He decided on a front pairing of Syd Puddefoot and Thomas Mitchell which many considered a gamble. While Puddefoot was already an accomplished striker, Mitchell had been moved from outside left, and was often said to lack the physical presence to play up front.

Nevertheless, Mitchell struck twice to sink Newcastle, aided by goals from his strike partner and one from George Thornewell on the right wing.

The fourth round trip to Exeter brought about Rovers' only slip-up along the road to Wembley. Crompton's side were expected to use this opportunity to end the barren spell with an emphatic win over the Division Three (South) side. However, goals from John Roscamp and Arthur Rigby were not enough as Exeter earned a creditable 2-2 draw. To make matters worse for Rovers, George Thornewell broke his collar bone, forcing him to miss the next two months of the season.

Left:
An advert endorsing the drinking of 'Oxo' by Blackburn Rovers' Club Secretary, from The Sports Telegraph dated Saturday April 21st 1928

Right:
Blackburn Rovers' 1928 Cup Winning Team, pictured here with the reserves and trophy

The replay at Ewood was no more encouraging. The 90 minutes could not separate the teams and Rovers fans were biting their nails as extra time arrived. However, Roscamp, Mitchell and Puddefoot provided a passage into the fifth round as the home side stumbled to a 3-1 win.

Crompton led Rovers into the home game against Port Vale on the back of a rare league win, again over Newcastle. While performances were far from impressive, the Blues were doing enough to keep themselves away from the threat of relegation.

It was another hard-fought victory in the freezing February conditions that saw Rovers through the fifth round. Another goal from Roscamp and Mitchell's last in the competition saw off Vale, but the Quarter Final draw brought the mighty Manchester United to Ewood.

Crompton knew his side could not go into the game against a club like United hoping to bounce back from a losing streak as they had in previous rounds. Sure enough, his side put together a run of three straight wins before the big day, the last FA Cup game of the season at Ewood.

United were not ignorant to this improved form, and decided to attempt to muscle their way through the tie, perhaps hoping to take Rovers back to Old Trafford and shoot them down in the replay. They concentrated their efforts on Puddefoot in particular, who was almost kicked off the park in an unpleasant encounter.

The Reds succeeded in cancelling Rovers out for a good 75 minutes of the game. However, the moment they eased off, Puddefoot took his chance, racing into the box to power a header into the back of the net.

A subdued United side could do nothing to stop the big forward now, and he did exactly the same minutes later to book Rovers a place in the Semi Finals.

A trip to Leicester's Filbert Street ground brought another stiff challenge in the form of Arsenal. The London giants were heavy favourites to progress to the Final, but in a tight affair it was Roscamp who scored the only goal to silence the Gunners fans and send the travelling Ewood faithful wild with delight.

Below:
Official club letterhead from 1913

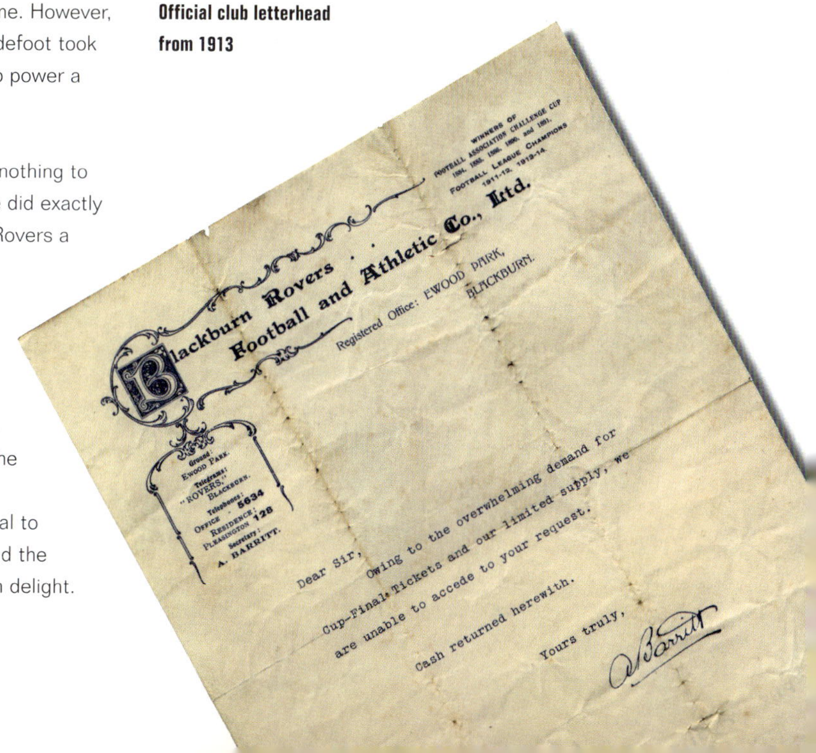
Blackburn Rovers Football and Athletic Co., Ltd.
Winners of Football Association Challenge Cup 1884, 1885, 1886, 1890, and 1891. Football League Champions 1911-12, 1913-14.
Registered Office: Ewood Park, Blackburn.
Ground: Ewood Park.
Telegrams: "Rovers," Blackburn.
Telephones: Office 5634. Residence: Pleasington 128.
Secretary: A. Barritt.

Dear Sir,
Owing to the overwhelming demand for Cup-Final Tickets and our limited supply, we are unable to accede to your request.
Cash returned herewith.
Yours truly,
A. Barritt

7 In what month in 1875 did the 17 founders of Blackburn Rovers meet at the St. Leger Hotel ?

(November)

Left:
The Cup Winning Team from 1928 pictured with trophy

Rovers were at Wembley again, but despite proving their doubters wrong time and time again along the way, Rovers were not fancied, not least because of some very poor league form. Eight defeats in eleven games, including a 6-0 defeat against Leicester on Rovers return to Filbert Street, had shattered confidence.

However, Crompton was not to be denied. He instilled a fighting spirit in his team rarely seen before or since.
Huddersfield came to Wembley confident of victory, despite the fact that they were one of few teams not to have beaten Rovers in the league all season.

All smiles before kick-off, Huddersfield were soon frowning as Roscamp raced through to score a controversial first minute goal.

After beating a defender, Roscamp charged after the ball, which Mercer in the Huddersfield goal stooped to collect on his line. However, a determined Roscamp simply steamrolled straight through the unsuspecting keeper, who, along with the ball, ended up in the back of the net!

Tommy McLean was the next to score for a rampant Rovers side. His powerful effort flew past Mercer, who was still shaken from the incident 21 minutes earlier with Roscamp.

Alec Jackson pulled one back for Huddersfield, who could have drawn level but for some sterling work from captain Harry Healless and Aussie Campbell at the back. Campbell was a rock in the heart of the Rovers defence throughout the 90 minutes, but it was Roscamp who had the final say, steering in his second of the game to seal the victory for Rovers.

Healless proudly held aloft the FA Cup for the last time in Rovers history, while Campbell marked the day by taking home the match ball.

Below:
Blackburn Rovers making Sunday morning front page headlines in the Sunday Graphic and Sunday Herald newspaper

Right:
Celebratory centre spread of the 1928 English Cup Final from The Weekly Telegraph

The following season Rovers' league form improved as Crompton managed to build on their cup success. Phenomenal crowds became the norm at Ewood and the record breaking 62,522 attendance against Bolton was a fitting tribute to what Crompton and his players had achieved.

Although the team gradually broke up, the spirit went on to inspire many future Rovers sides.

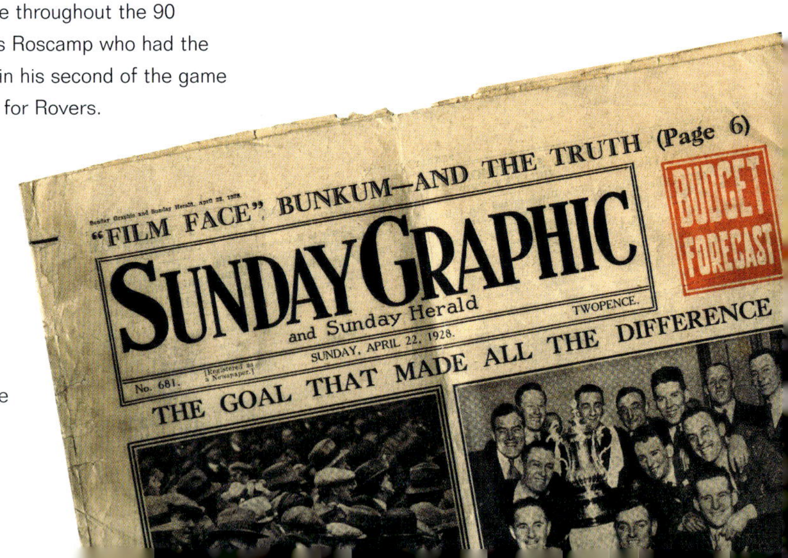
"FILM FACE" BUNKUM—AND THE TRUTH (Page 6)

BUDGET FORECAST

SUNDAY GRAPHIC
and Sunday Herald

No. 681. SUNDAY, APRIL 22, 1928. TWOPENCE.

THE GOAL THAT MADE ALL THE DIFFERENCE

THE WEEKLY TELEGRAPH.
Twopence, Weekly.
The Weekly Telegraph, April 21, 1928

£1,000 MUST-BE-WON CUP FINAL COMPETITION.
CLOSING DATE, THURSDAY, APRIL 19.

ON SALE TO-DAY.

Headline Stories

1938-39 – Promotion To Division One

Nothing gives a football manager more pleasure than to prove people wrong.

Just last year, former England boss Graham Taylor ignored years of ridicule to take lowly Watford to the Premiership.

Before that there was Sir Alex Ferguson, now the darling of the Manchester United fans who once called for his head. And, long before all that, there was Bob Crompton.

Forced out of his role as Rovers manager in 1931, Crompton spent years on the Rovers board, watching as the club slipped out of the top flight for the first time in its proud history.

It would not be long, however, before he was king of Ewood Park once more.

Although it was ultimately his decision to cease managerial activities, his departure followed an official complaint from the playing staff to the chairman regarding Crompton's style.

However, after the club was relegated to the Second Division, Crompton was reinstated to his former post in May 1938.

A stubborn man of firm beliefs, his iron-handed approach was not always welcomed by the players who learned not to question the great man.

The first game of the season showed much promise. Over 15,000 fans watched as Albert Clarke, signed by Crompton from Birmingham, netted twice and Billy Guest completed a 3-2 win over Tranmere Rovers at Ewood Park. Two days later Billy Rogers and Len Butt made certain of a 2-1 victory over West Ham at Upton Park, and Rovers were flying high.

September brought two away games in five days, and although Rovers earned a creditable 2-0 win at Chesterfield thanks to goals from Walter Crook and Rogers, by the time they played Sheffield Wednesday at Hillsborough the players were too tired from travelling to make it four wins out of four.

A 3-0 defeat laid to rest any hopes of a memorable 100% run, but that is not to say the season did not prove to be memorable in itself.

Quite the opposite in fact. Two 4-0 wins over Swansea and Bradford and a 3-1 victory over West Ham kept Rovers at the top of the league, just seven games into one of the greatest nine months in the club's illustrious history. However, the next four games saw Rovers take a solitary point, putting a dampener on any premature promotion parties.

8 Which goalkeeper was also the club's first captain?

(Thomas Greenwood)

9 What was Rovers' first ground called?

(The Oozehead Ground)

11 Which club did Rovers beat 7-3 in April 1881?

(Sheffield Wednesday)

Left:
The 1939 Blackburn Rovers' Team

Right:
Blackburn player Robert Tomlinson

Far Right:
A letter dated 1945 from Rovers' club secretary, enquiring if Tomlinson was able to get leave, enabling him to play over the Christmas period

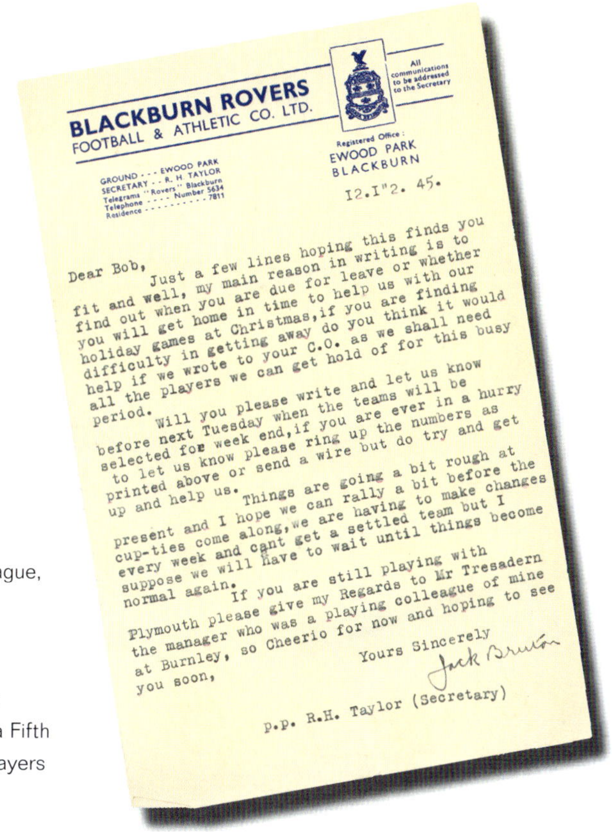

BLACKBURN ROVERS
FOOTBALL & ATHLETIC CO. LTD.

All communications to be addressed to the Secretary

GROUND - - - EWOOD PARK
SECRETARY - - R. H. TAYLOR
Telegrams "Rovers" Blackburn
Telephone - - - - Number 5634
Residence - - - - - - - - - 7811

Registered Office :
EWOOD PARK
BLACKBURN

I2.I"2. 45.

Dear Bob,
Just a few lines hoping this finds you fit and well, my main reason in writing is to find out when you are due for leave or whether you will get home in time to help us with our holiday games at Christmas,if you are finding difficulty in getting away do you think it would help if we wrote to your C.O. as we shall need all the players we can get hold of for this busy period.

Will you please write and let us know before next Tuesday when the teams will be selected for week end,if you are ever in a hurry to let us know please ring up the numbers as printed above or send a wire but do try and get up and help us.

Things are going a bit rough at present and I hope we can rally a bit before the cup-ties come along,we are having to make changes every week and cant get a settled team but I suppose we will have to wait until things become normal again.

If you are still playing with Plymouth please give my Regards to Mr Tresadern the manager who was a playing colleague of mine at Burnley, so Cheerio for now and hoping to see you soon,

Yours Sincerely
Jack Bruton

P.P. R.H. Taylor (Secretary)

Crompton was as business like as always in his efforts to halt the slide. A quick return to winning ways against Tottenham lifted the players spirits, but a draw at Luton and a home defeat by Coventry put paid to any danger of the players becoming over-confident. By this time, they shared their manager's no-nonsense approach and were prepared to buckle down and make sure Rovers soon returned to Division One.

Nottingham Forest were the unfortunate side on the receiving end of Rovers' new workman-like approach. Crompton's side ground out an impressive 3-1 win at the City Ground, followed by a 3-0 win over Newcastle at Ewood Park which included a hat-trick from Clarke, who had already bagged 15 goals by the tail end of November.

A disappointing 2-0 defeat at West Brom was followed by a fantastic 6-0 win over Norwich at Ewood.

Southampton and Plymouth were both beaten convincingly before Rovers only managed a draw against Tranmere. However, it turned out to be nothing but a hiccup as Crompton watched his team march to three successive wins as 1938 drew to a close. Bury were beaten twice and the trip to Chesterfield saw Clarke back on the goal trail with his first in six games.

A home defeat at the hands of Sheffield Wednesday on January 2nd gave Rovers a disappointing start to 1939, but they bounced back in style five days later, beating Swansea 2-0 at Ewood Park in the FA Cup Third round.

Swansea got their revenge in the league, however, beating Rovers 2-1.

Southend were the next team to be knocked off the cup trail by rampant Rovers, a 4-2 win enough to set up a Fifth round tie against Sunderland. The players were not too drained for the visit of Bradford two days later, a 6-4 win entertaining the fans, but a leaky defence proving a worry for Crompton.

That point was highlighted in Rovers next league fixture, away at Manchester City. A 3-2 defeat left Crompton fuming and the players ears stinging. It did the trick, though, as the next game at home to Millwall saw Rovers take two valuable points, and concede just once in a 3-1 win.

The FA Cup trip to Roker Park now beckoned, and Rovers defence held up bravely again, just one lapse making the final score 1-1, setting up an Ewood replay five days later. However, despite Rovers first clean sheet of the year, they failed to score, meaning a second replay would have to decide the tie.

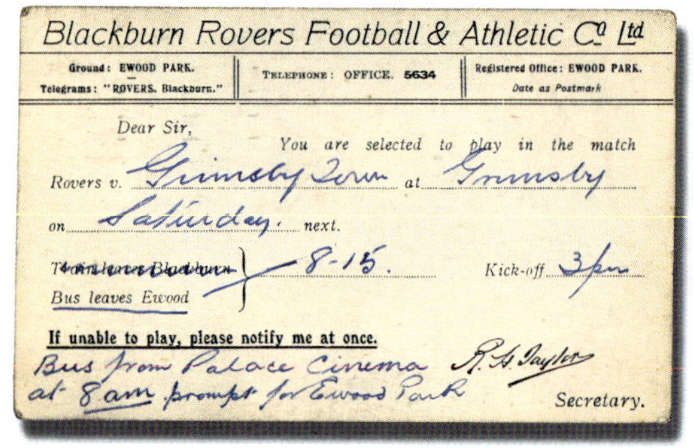

Blackburn Rovers Football & Athletic Co Ltd

Ground: EWOOD PARK. Telegrams: "ROVERS, Blackburn." | TELEPHONE: OFFICE. 5634 | Registered Office: EWOOD PARK. Date as Postmark

Dear Sir,

You are selected to play in the match Rovers v. Grimsby Town at Grimsby on Saturday next.

Train leaves Blackburn 8-15. Kick-off 3pm
Bus leaves Ewood

If unable to play, please notify me at once.

Bus from Palace Cinema at 8am prompt for Ewood Park

R. G. Taylor
Secretary.

Left:
Postcard from 1945.
Notification to team member of selection to play against Grimsby Town at home

Exhausted, Rovers could manage only a 1-0 win over local rivals Burnley before travelling to Hillsborough for the all important cup tie, their fourth match in ten days. More than 30,000 fans saw Rovers scrape through with a 1-0 win thanks to a goal from Guest, only his second of the season.

After their cup heroics Rovers' defence could hold out no longer and the trip to White Hart Lane saw Tottenham run out 4-3 winners. To make matters worse, Rovers lost full-back Billy Hough for the rest of the season through injury. As people began to seriously question Rovers' credentials as title hopefuls, they managed only a 1-1 draw in the FA Cup sixth round at Huddersfield. The return game heralded the end of Rovers brave, but tiring, cup run, Town emerging 2-1 victors to secure a place in the semi-finals.

Just two days after their cup exit it was Coventry who felt the backlash, a single Butt goal enough to give Rovers a league victory at Highfield Road.

After that, four goals in two games from Jock Weddle helped Crompton's side to three straight league wins. Weddle was again on target at St. James' Park as Newcastle were held to a 2-2 draw.

With just seven league games left to play, Rovers were in impressive form and looked all set for a return to Division One after a three year absence. Sure enough, two more wins followed, West Brom defeated 3-0 and a well-earned 3-2 victory at Fulham seemed to have set Rovers up for another good run.

However, a shock 4-0 defeat at Norwich left Rovers fans reeling, especially since the Ewood fixture had finished so emphatically in Rovers favour. As they prayed for a swift return to form, Rovers' title rivals were praying for just the opposite, but fortunately Rovers managed to grind out a win, Fulham again making life difficult as a 2-1 win at Ewood kept the blue flag flying.

Rovers seemed to have got back into their stride with a 3-0 win against Southampton, but it was to be the last time Rovers were to score that season.

After a 1-0 defeat at Plymouth, a 0-0 draw at Sheffield United was enough to keep Rovers at the top, bring the title trophy to Ewood Park and to send Crompton and his players back into Division One.

Rovers front line was the toast of the town, Clarke finishing the season with 21 goals while Weddle, Rogers and Butt were not far behind in the scoring stakes.

But the true hero stayed out of the limelight. The man who had masterminded the whole thing and to whom the town owed so much was happy to let his players wallow in the glory.

10 Which Scottish side did Rovers face at Alexandra Meadows on January 2nd, 1878?
(Partick Thistle)

12 Who beat Rovers 1-0 in the 1882 FA Cup final?
(Old Etonians)

13 In which round of the 1882-83 FA Cup were Rovers eliminated?
(Second)

14 In which year did Jimmy Forrest join Rovers?
(1883)

Headline Stories

1959-60 - FA Cup Final

Right:
Cup Final Songsheet for BRFC v Wolverhampton Wanderers at Wembley Stadium Saturday May 7 1960

Left:
Blackburn Rovers supporters in cheerful mood as they pass Buckingham Palace during a morning sightseeing tour of London before going on to Wembley for the FA Cup Final.

No football experience can quite match that of an FA Cup Final.

In terms of magical atmospheres it has no equal . . . the dream fixture for all players and all fans.

Rovers six FA Cup wins occurred in the club's first 53 years (1875-1928), well outside living memory for the majority, making the events of a spring afternoon in 1960 all the more disappointing.

After decades of Semi-Final exits, Sixth Round replay defeats and even the odd Third Round setback, this was going to be the moment Rovers fans had craved for decades. If only.

Dally Duncan was the man who led Rovers to Wembley. Brought in to replace Johnny Carey, who had left for Everton, Duncan did not have it easy, presiding over a disastrous injury and illness crisis.

One by one his first choice team evaporated as the opening weeks of the season took their toll. But, remarkably, Duncan managed to inspire Rovers to four wins from their first five games!

Fulham were on the wrong end of a 4-0 first day win courtesy of two goals from Derek Dougan and one each from Roy Vernon and Peter Dobing.

However, Rovers hero Bryan Douglas became the season's first casualty, missing the next three games. Home and away victories against Bolton followed either side of a 2-2 draw at Nottingham Forest, but by the time September arrived Rovers had lost keeper Harry Leyland and forward Roy Vernon.

A 3-1 victory over Sheffield Wednesday was followed by back-to-back league defeats at the hands of Wolves and Everton.

But as Rovers were to find out that the first defeat of the season was not to be the most painful the Molineux outfit were to inflict!

After a poor yield of three points from six games, three straight wins over Leicester, Burnley and Leeds - all by a one goal margin - saw Rovers hanging on amongst the leading teams in the country, but by no means convincingly.

By now the team was virtually unrecognisable from the one that started the season. Full back Ken Taylor faced months on the sidelines, and was replaced by John Bray. Douglas, who had only been back in the side for a handful of games, was starting his second injury layoff of the season. Vernon, who was still working his way back to fitness, was about to suffer an injury which would keep him out until the New Year.

November saw a weakened Rovers side remain strong at home, beating West Brom and Birmingham. However, without several influential players the team could not pick up a point on their travels.

Chelsea, Newcastle and Tottenham all enjoyed home wins against Rovers, and it seemed as if the club were destined never to record another away win.

However, the first day hammering of Fulham proved too much of a psychological edge, and coming off the back of an impressive 6-2 home win over West Ham, a single Dougan goal was enough to put a temporary end to Rovers awful away form. Dougan gave Rovers the points once again as Blackpool were defeated, but despite having managed eleven goals so far, he was to net just three more in the league all season as the inevitable happened and Rovers began to sink down the table.

The club failed to record back-to-back league wins throughout the second half of the campaign, but by now the magic of the FA Cup was proving too much of a distraction for that to dampen the supporters' spirits.

Rovers did not start the competition too convincingly. A Dobing goal at Sunderland spared a third round exit, but the replay saw Rovers win comfortably with Vernon on target twice and Ally MacLeod and Louis Bimpson netting the others.

Vernon's brace turned out to be his last goals for the club, Everton providing the striker with a route out of Ewood Park. Vernon went on to score a ton of goals in five years at Goodison Park, but not only did he miss out on Rovers' Cup Final outing, he also left Everton two years before they reached the final in 1966.

15 By what score did Rovers beat Sheffield Park Grange in October 1884, 8-0, 12-0 or 17-0?
(17-0)

16 In what year was the Nuttall Street Stand constructed, 1902, 1906 or 1909?
(1906)

Left:
Unlucky Mick McGrath, puts the ball into his own goal in the 1960 FA Cup Final at Wembley

Right:
Blackburn Rovers' Season Ticket 1947-48

Rovers again needed a replay to progress to the Fifth round after a 1-1 draw at home to Blackpool. The return match at Bloomfield Road saw Rovers see off their opponents with a couple from Dobing and one from Dougan.

Rovers recorded a rare league win over Manchester City before meeting Spurs in the fifth round. No replay was necessary this time however, as Bimpson added two goals to Woods' opener to send the Ewood stars into the Quarter Finals.

The league was a different story. The Rovers side who lost a First Division fixture 4-1 to Spurs seemed nothing like the same one that had beaten the London side so emphatically just a week earlier.

Rovers then conceded a total of six goals in two defeats by local rivals Burnley and Preston, before returning to Turf Moor, home of their greatest rivals, for the Quarter Final.

After a baffling run of form in which Rovers seemed to distance themselves completely from their league performances, it appeared Rovers FA Cup luck had finally deserted them. With just 17 minutes on the clock Duncan's team were three down and all but out.

However, when Rovers were awarded a dubious penalty for handball, Douglas took the opportunity to score what most people still saw as little more than a consolation goal. Three minutes later, the Clarets were starting to panic as Dobing smashed home a 25-yard drive that had the departing Rovers fans scurrying back to their seats.

Rovers laid siege on the home goal and Burnley finally cracked open for a third time. There was a touch of good fortune about it, a speculative effort from Ronnie Clayton rebounding off a Burnley defender into the path of Mick McGrath, who could not believe his luck as his sliced shot found the back of the net.

A crowd of 53,000 gathered for the replay and extra-time goals from Dobing and McLeod finished off the Clarets.

A Semi-Final date with Sheffield Wednesday beckoned, but first there was the small task of maintaining First Division status. A defeat at West Ham was not what the doctor had ordered and the situation was seriously worrying.

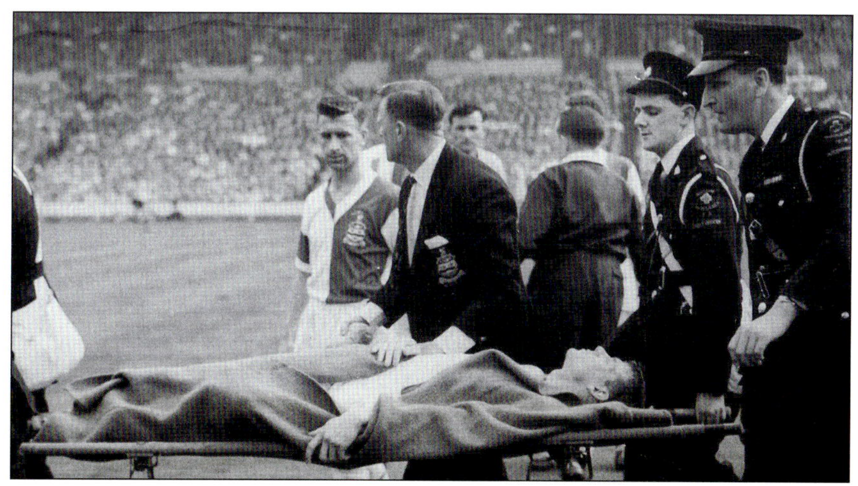

Left:
Dave Whelan, Blackburn's left back, is stretchered off with a severely broken leg after a clash with Norman Deeley

17 From which London club was goalkeeper Jimmy Ashcroft brought to Ewood Park?
(Woolwich Arsenal)

18 In which year did Rovers first win the league championship?
(1912)

**Right:
BRFC Captain,
Ronnie Clayton
watches commentator
David Coleman
interview Wolves'
Bill Slater**

Had Rovers not been involved in the Cup, many reckon Duncan would have lost his job.

Derek Dougan was the Rovers hero against Wednesday - how that was to change!- the leggy striker taking his season's tally to 17 with a brace.

Dougan helped Rovers scramble eight points from their final last nine games to secure top flight status before he rocked the club with a transfer request on the morning of the Final itself. If maximum impact was his goal then he certainly achieved it.

Dougan's desire to leave the club was expressed too late for him not to be included in the starting eleven. It was to prove just one in a succession of Wembley disasters for Rovers.

McGrath, hero against Burnley in the Quarter-Final, put through his own goal to give Wolves the perfect start. Just a minute later, Whelan clashed with Norman Deeley and was stretchered off with a severely broken leg.

Things went from bad to worse to terrible and two further goals destroyed any hopes ten man Rovers had of salvaging anything from the game.

Rovers' fans, so vociferous, excited and optimistic beforehand, were reduced to tears of despair. Duncan took the brunt of the criticism and, after refusing to resign, he was sacked.

19 From which Scottish club did Rovers sign Percy Dawson for £2,500?
(Hearts)

20 Who was Rovers first full-time manager?
(Jack Carr)

WHEN IT COMES TO QUALITY USED CARS...
...WE'RE IN A LEAGUE OF OUR OWN!!
AUTODROME
AUTODROME... THE USED CAR CHAMPIONS
Clio
MICRA
Saxo
ALWAYS OVER 100 QUALITY VEHICLES ON SITE
AUTO DROME
Junction 6
M65
ACCRINGTON ROAD
TESCO
FIAT
RENAULT
TOYOTA
ATS
WE ARE HERE
AUTO DROME
HOTLINE 01254 680441
PENDLE ST • COPY NOOK • BLACKBURN
OPENING TIMES: Mon-Fri 9am-7pm. Sat 9am-6pm. Sun 11am-5pm

Headline Stories

1974-75 - Third Division Champions

Compared to winning the Premiership title or the FA Cup, claiming the Third Division title hardly rates as a major achievement.

But do not try telling that to the fans who followed Rovers, under the expert guidance of Gordon Lee, in the season 1974-75.

After so many years on a starvation diet, this was caviar and champagne for supporters hungry for something to shout about.

Lee had brought in five new players during pre-season, two of them, Ken Beamish and Graham Oates, scoring on their debuts to give Rovers a 2-1 first day victory over Grimsby.

Beamish was again on target in the 2-0 League Cup win at Stockport while Oates grabbed his second for the club in the 3-2 home league win over Colchester. Sadly though the trip to Swindon ended in defeat, Rovers going down 2-0.

Rovers were soon back to winning ways against Brighton as a single Don Martin goal proved enough to give Rovers the points. Lee's side then earned a League Cup second round replay after a 2-2 draw at Northampton.

Left: 1974/75 Third Division Champions from L to R : Derek Fazackerley, Ken Beamish, Gordon Lee and Tony Parkes, all celebrate in the dressing room

Right:
Gordon Lee arriving at Ewood Park

A 0-0 draw at Preston North End was followed by a 1-0 cup win over Northampton. Then Oates scored the deciding goals in important single goal successes against Halifax and Southend.

Rovers picked up their second draw of the season at Tranmere before enjoying a 4-1 victory which included a fine hat-trick from Martin. Three days later, Oates was again the scorer in a 1-0 win, this time over Bournemouth at Ewood Park.

Rovers then travelled to Fourth Division Hartlepool for a League Cup Third round tie, but could only manage a draw. Following that, Chesterfield were beaten 2-1, but the return match with Hartlepool turned out to be the low point of Rovers' season, a Tony Parkes goal not enough as 'Pool snatched a shock 2-1 victory.

A double from Beamish earned a point at home to Port Vale, but Rovers were beaten again three days later, Crystal Palace inflicting a 1-0 defeat at Selhurst Park, before Rovers finally picked up two valuable points away at Walsall.

A Beamish strike gave Rovers the points at Bury before a goal from John Waddington earned a draw at home to Crystal Palace. Rovers lost to Peterborough United before Martin sealed two points at home to Aldershot with a double strike, and lowly Matlock Town were dumped out of the FA Cup with a 4-1 away win.

But a run of just two points from four games, including defeats at Charlton and Hereford, left Rovers clinging on to top spot by the skin of their teeth, despite the fact that they had beaten Darlington in the FA Cup. Arch rivals Plymouth were now looking the stronger side and were seriously challenging Lee's side for the title.

Rovers bought themselves a little breathing space with three straight league wins against Preston, Huddersfield and Charlton, but Plymouth were still snapping at their heels.

The South Coast side took their opportunity as Rovers reeled from a disappointing FA Cup defeat by Bristol Rovers. A 0-0 draw with Watford was followed by another defeat by Peterborough, before the unthinkable happened.

Rovers travelled to Plymouth and despite a Beamish goal they went down 2-1 to lose their grip on top spot.

Jimmy Mullen's broken leg, sustained against Peterborough, left Rovers short in midfield but Lee acted quickly, swooping to sign Grimsby's Mike Hickman for £10,000.

21 In what year was Jack Carr appointed manager of Rovers?
(1922)

22 Bob Crompton became club secretary in 1921 - true or false?
(False - he became a director)

Hickman kicked off his Rovers career in a three man attack when Lee's side made the short trip to neighbours Bury. Despite going a goal down, Hickman became an instant hero, heading Rovers level before Martin rounded off the scoring to give Rovers a priceless win.

However, when Plymouth came to Ewood, fans had their heads in their hands again as Rovers went 2-0 down inside 20 minutes. Beamish managed to pull one back before half time, but it looked as if Plymouth were about to pull away at the top.

Lee was having none of it. We will never know what was said in the half time team-talk, but Rovers played with more passion and commitment in the second half than they had all season.

Two goals each for Martin and Hickman sent the Ewood hordes into raptures and the Pilgrims returned home with their tails between their legs. More importantly, it put Rovers back on top.

Rovers then went on a strange run, taking wins and draws from alternate games. This continued from mid-February to early April, when four successive draws, including a 3-3 thriller at home to Walsall, left Rovers with just four games left to play.

The first was against Chesterfield. A convincing display saw Stuart Metcalfe and Hickman sink the Spireites and secure promotion for Rovers. But the celebrations were put on hold with Lee setting his sights on the title.

Plymouth, who had achieved promotion a few days earlier, were not about to give up either.

Rovers did suffer a minor hangover in the next game, beaten 2-0 at Colchester, but Lee's team were still in pole position and a trip to Port Vale saw Rovers stamp their authority on the league and pencil their name into the record books. Fazackerley, Metcalfe and Hickman added to a Dave Harris own goal to give Rovers a 4-1 victory.

As news filtered through that Peterborough had defeated Plymouth, jubilant Rovers fans realised that only a mathematical miracle on the last day of the season could rob them of the title now.

A point was all they needed at home to Wrexham and that was just what they got. A 0-0 draw was something of an anti-climax, but the Ewood faithful didn't seem to mind. The result was forgotten as the promotion party got underway.

Right:
Cult hero,
David Speedie

Headline Stories

1991-92 – Promotion Via Wembley

Right:
The triumphant
Rovers celebrate
promotion to the
Premier League

Enter Jack Walker.

Officially involved since 1991, Mr Walker totally changed the face of football at Ewood Park to set the famous club on the road to ultimate glory.

He totally changed the face of football at Ewood Park and set the famous club on the road to the ultimate glory.

Languishing at the wrong end of Division Two, having spent the previous season flirting with relegation, Rovers parted company with manager Don MacKay and replaced him with Kenny Dalglish.

It was to prove a master stroke.

Dalglish, already a world soccer legend, received a rapturous reception minutes before the game against Plymouth Argyle. The great man's impact was instant as Rovers won 5-2.

The only way was up.

Dalglish had left Liverpool months earlier, claiming he had retired due to the stress of management. However, the challenge of leading an 'unfashionable' club back to the big time was too much for the Scot to resist.

In his first four games Dalglish led Rovers to eight points and they began to climb the table. He was active off the pitch too, completing transfer deals to recruit full-back Alan Wright from Blackpool as well as former Ewood favourite Colin Hendry, who returned from Manchester City.

Both players were part of the team that beat Charlton 2-0 and by the time Barnsley visited Ewood Park Rovers' transfer record had been smashed with the signing of Mike Newell from Everton. His £1.1 million fee was the first seven-figure sum Rovers had paid out - but certainly not the last.

Newell scored Rovers third in a 3-0 win to become an instant hit with the fans, who saw him form an impressive partnership with cult hero David Speedie up front. Drogheda United midfielder Gary Tallon was brought in along with Aston Villa playmaker Gordon Cowans as Rovers' expenditure figure rose almost as quickly as the club's league standing.

By mid-December Rovers found themselves third in Division Two. Unfortunately, the season's low point arrived just as Rovers should have been celebrating their highest position for years, chairman Bill Fox sadly passing away before he had a chance to see his team promoted.

Over the next couple of months Rovers were irresistible, scoring for fun and giving nothing away at the back. Hendry was fast becoming an Ewood legend again while Newell and Speedie had developed an unrivalled understanding.

Unfortunately, it was following an injury to Newell that Rovers form fell away. Poised at the top of the division and looking certainties for the title, Dalglish's side rectified a bad patch with a 3-0 win over struggling Brighton. This though, was followed by a run of six straight defeats, and before long Rovers had plummeted into seventh position.

Above Left: Colin Hendry and Kevin Moran celebrating in the Semi-Final playoff against Derby

23 What was Rovers' final league position at the end of the 1902-03 season 8th, 12th or 16th ?
(16th)

24 Which Rovers player was killed while fighting in World War One?
(Eddie Latheron)

25 Who was Rovers top scorer in the championship winning season of 1911-12?
(Walter Aitkenhead)

26 Which Rovers player scored four goals in a 6-0 win over Bolton in October 1912?
(William Cameron)

Right: The controversial penalty, David Speedie on the floor in the match against Leicester

In Newell's absence, Dalglish brought in Swindon striker Duncan Shearer.

Despite a goal on his debut, Shearer never quite lived up to expectations, and Newell was welcomed back into the team alongside Speedie in April.

A slight improvement in form left Rovers in with a chance of securing a play-off place if they could beat Plymouth on the last day of the season. Fortunately, results went their way, and Rovers scraped into the top six with a 3-1 win, thanks to a hat-trick from Speedie which also relegated the South Coast side.

Obviously Rovers would have preferred to go up automatically, not least because they had suffered so much play-off heartache over the past few years.

However, Derby, who Rovers would play in a two-legged semi final, had already been beaten twice that season. Two Derby goals in the first 15 minutes at Ewood Park left Rovers facing an uphill struggle to survive the tie. Scott Sellars pulled a goal back just after the half-hour mark but it seemed little more than a consolation.

Mike Newell changed all that with a fierce strike just before half time to blow the game wide open again.

In the second half Rovers took full control, two Speedie goals giving Dalglish's side a 4-2 lead to take to the Baseball Ground. It could have been more, Rovers playing with an energy that had been missing from their play for months, but had suddenly come flooding back to bury a stunned Derby side.

Despite a Kevin Moran goal Rovers lost the second leg 2-1, but a trip to Wembley was safely in the bag.

27 From which club did Rovers sign three players in February 1908?
(Brighton & Hove Albion)

28 Which inside-forward cost just £25 when he signed from Grangetown in March 1906?
(Eddie Latheron)

29 Which Rover won his first England cap in May 1902?
(Bob Crompton)

Left:
Mike Newell scores the winning goal from the penalty spot

Leicester provided the opposition for Rovers' first visit to the national stadium since the 1987 Full Members Cup win. A typical Wembley final, the game was hard-fought with neither team giving much away until, on the stroke of half-time, Speedie went sprawling in the box under a challenge from Steve Walsh. Referee George Courtney immediately awarded the penalty, to the amazement of the Leicester players who felt Speedie had made the most of the challenge.

Newell placed the ball on the spot and ignored the whistles and jeers of the Leicester supporters to send Carl Muggleton the wrong way and give Rovers the lead.

The second half saw Dalglish's side bombarded with wave after wave of Leicester attacks. Somehow, Bobby Mimms' goal remained intact, and Rovers were even awarded a second penalty on a rare excursion forward but this time Newell was denied by Muggleton.

It made no difference as Rovers held out for the narrowest of victories to secure promotion to the all-new Premier League.

Rovers, who had played in their all-yellow change kit, quickly reverted to their traditional blue and white halves for the post-match celebrations, although in truth few fans noticed amidst the euphoria. The look of delight on Jack Walker's face was clear to see as he congratulated captain Kevin Moran on the Wembley steps.

"Rovers were back in the big time... the start of a wonderful journey"

Headline Stories

1994-95 - Premier League Champions

When the FA Premier League was formed in 1992, Alex Ferguson had already moulded his Manchester United side into the best in the country.

Despite losing the title race to Leeds the previous season (while Rovers were busy winning promotion) few argued that United were the team to beat and they proved popular opinion to be correct by claiming the first two Premier League titles.

No-one would have bet against them winning a third. Their closest rivals from the previous season were Rovers, who had impressed everyone with their meteoric rise.

Jack Walker's capital investment had given Kenny Dalglish colossal spending power but could they out-fight and out-smart mighty United?

If the Charity Shield was anything to go by, then the answer had to be no.

Dalglish found himself without the services of star striker Alan Shearer, £5 million record summer signing from Norwich, Chris Sutton, as well as fellow frontrunner Mike Newell. With Kevin Gallacher and Paul Warhurst joining David Batty on the long-term casualty list, the team was desperately short in attack. Depleted Rovers found United too strong and slumped to a 2-0 defeat.

However, Rovers began the league season in fine form. The SAS strikeforce of Shearer and Sutton quickly gelled into the most potent attacking partnership in the country.

The opening match was tight, a single Shearer goal giving Rovers the points at the expense of his former club, Southampton.

The visit of Leicester City to Ewood Park did live up to expectations. Sutton's first goal for the club 18 minutes into his home debut set Rovers on their way to a 3-0 win, with Henning Berg and Shearer adding a goal each.

Above: Stuart Ripley in action

Right: Jack Walker stands proud after watching his team win the Premiership Trophy

Rovers then played hosts to perennial relegation scrappers Coventry, who were sent home battered and bruised from a 4-0 defeat which included a superb Sutton hat-trick.

A 0-0 draw with Arsenal at Highbury followed, before Rovers were back on the winning trail with a 3-0 win over Everton. However, disaster struck in Rovers first ever UEFA Cup match. What was seen as an easy game at home to Swedish part-timers Trelleborgs turned out to be a shambles, with the visitors coming away from Ewood Park with a 1-0 victory.

After a narrow 2-1 win over Chelsea, Birmingham were beaten in the first leg of the Coca-Cola Cup second round. The SAS shot down Aston Villa with a 3-1 win, before Dalglish's side travelled to Sweden to settle the score with Trelleborgs.

Left:
The Premiership winning team

Bottom Left:
Tim Sherwood gets his hands on the Premiership trophy

Goals from Shearer and Sutton seemed to have given Rovers a 2-1 win, which would have seen them through on away goals but an equaliser in the dying minutes sent Trelleborgs into the second round and a mouth-watering tie against Italian giants Lazio.

Eight games into the season the bookies were already billing Rovers as favourites for the title, despite their European howler.

Dalglish's multi-million pound strikeforce was still firing on all cylinders. New boy Sutton had seven goals, while Shearer was not far behind with six.

However, despite an early goal against his old club, Sutton could not prevent his side going down to their first defeat of the season at Norwich. He did rescue a draw with a second half strike against Birmingham in the second leg of the Coca-Cola Cup tie, but it was down to Shearer to earn Rovers a point from the penalty spot against his home-town club, Newcastle.

After three domestic games without a win, Rovers were back in business against Liverpool. A close game saw Mark Atkins score Rovers' first with Sutton adding two to seal a 3-2 win despite a spectacular John Barnes goal.

With a sound win under their belts Rovers were confident and raring to go as champions United finally visited Ewood. Paul Warhurst's 40-yard effort gave Dalglish's side the perfect start, but disaster struck shortly before half time, when Henning Berg collided with Lee Sharpe in the Rovers area.

Replays showed that Berg had played the ball first, but amazingly the referee awarded a penalty and showed the Norwegian defender the red card in a double disaster for Dalglish's team. Eric Cantona confidently placed the ball past Tim Flowers to level the scores.

Rovers fought bravely and Colin Hendry headed home to restore the lead, but the pressure told and United scored three times to take all the points. Two Shearer goals saw Coventry knocked out of the Coca Cola Cup in the third round as Rovers bounced straight back from a difficult few weeks. A 2-0 win over Nottingham Forest turned out to be the first of eight straight league victories, a run which included an impressive 4-0 home win over QPR, in which Alan Shearer scored his first hat-trick of the season.

Unfortunately midway through the run Dalglish saw his old club Liverpool end Rovers Coca Cola Cup run with a 3-1 win at Ewood.

A disappointing goalless draw with Leicester followed, before three wins over Manchester City, Crystal Palace and West Ham took Rovers to an impressive record of 31 points from a possible 33 since the end of October.

As January drew to a close the FA Cup beckoned. Rovers found Newcastle too strong to beat at Ewood Park, and the replay at St. James' left Rovers with just the league to play for. Nottingham Forest had already been beaten for the second time before Manchester United once again provided the opposition, this time at Old Trafford.

Determined to pay United back for the defeat at Ewood, Rovers were heartbroken when Cantona put United one up. Rovers thought they had equalised when captain Tim Sherwood headed the ball past Peter Schmeichel late but referee Paul Durkin ruled it out for a foul by Shearer.

Rovers bounced straight back from that controversial and potentially crippling defeat to beat Ipswich 4-1, largely thanks to another Shearer hat-trick. However, a 1-1 draw against Leeds (Tim Flowers was sent off, Alan Shearer scored a penalty and the Yorkshire club equalised all in the first 10 minutes!) and an away defeat at the hands of Tottenham showed that cracks were starting to appear.

Dalglish was quick to act and home wins over Sheffield Wednesday and Wimbledon put Rovers right back on track.

A 0-0 draw against Norwich was only the fourth time Rovers had failed to score all season. Aston Villa and Arsenal were both beaten before a 1-1 draw at Highfield Road against struggling Coventry.

Chelsea were disposed of at Stamford Bridge and two straight away wins at Everton and QPR followed before a single Hendry goal earned a 1-1 draw at Leeds. The title race was really hotting up with Rovers in pole position and United struggling to keep up.

**Centre:
Shearer and Sutton celebrate their team's victory**

**Facing Page:
Jack Walker congratulates Alan Shearer**

asics
McEWAN'S
LAGER
CARLING

Right:
Colin Hendry with Trophy and medal

Suddenly and without any good reason, Rovers' form began to slip. Despite goals from Shearer and Hendry, Manchester City came away from Ewood Park with a 3-2 win. Rovers then struggled to over-come Crystal Palace. New signing Jeff Kenna scored his first goal for the club and although Kevin Gallacher came back from a long term injury to make it 2-1, he was later carried off with a broken leg.

West Ham then proved too much for a Rovers side who were visibly feeling the strain, the Hammers winning 2-0 at Upton Park.

Rovers were accused of lacking the "bottle" to win the Championship ahead of the final home game of the season against in-form Newcastle. But in Shearer, Rovers had the ultimate weapon. The phenomenal striker was once again on target against his old club while England colleague Flowers pulled off several tremendous saves to deny the visitors.

United beat Coventry, thanks to a double from Andy Cole, to take the title race to the season's final day.

Rovers, with an advantage of two points, faced Liverpool at Anfield - scene of so many glory days for Dalglish - while United were given the comparatively easy task of defeating West Ham at Upton Park.

Dalglish's side made the best possible start, Shearer - who else? - striding onto a cross from Stuart Ripley to slam the ball home much to the delight of supporters at both ends. Many of the Anfield regulars had turned up in Rovers shirts, praying that United would not make it three titles in a row!

But there was no danger of the Liverpool players rolling over and giving Rovers an easy ride to the title. Another great cheer went up around the stadium as news filtered through that United had fallen behind at West Ham, but the smiles soon turned to worrying frowns as Barnes equalised for Liverpool. To make matters worse, Anfield soon became aware that United had equalised too.

Sutton had a shot cleared off the line and, down at Upton Park, Andy Cole missed a golden opportunity before the final goal of the day left fans around the country on the edge of their seats.

Jamie Redknapp fired in a free kick from the edge of the area to give Liverpool the lead, but seconds later it was the Rovers fans who were raising the roof as they were told that the final whistle had been blown at Upton Park.

Rovers had done it - their first title in 81 years. Just four years after struggling at the foot of the old Division Two. Kenny Dalglish's Ewood revolution was complete.

A banner in the crowd said it all - Blackburn Rovers, Champions of England.

Headline Stories

Supporting Features

FA Cup:

Winners in 1883-84 beating Queen's Park (Glasgow) 2-1, 1884-85 beating Queen's Park (Glasgow) 2-0, 1885-86 beating West Brom 2-0 after a replay, 1889-90 beating Sheffield Wednesday 6-1 and 1890-91 beating Notts County 3-1.
(Rovers were beaten finalists in 1881-82, losing 0-1 to Old Etonians).

Promotion:

As runners up in old Division Two under Johnny Carey in 1957-58, clinching promotion by winning 4-3 at Charlton in front of 56,435 on the final day.

As runners up in old Division Three under player-manager Howard Kendall in 1979-80, a season which included a memorable run of 15 games - 14 wins and one draw between mid January and mid April.

Charity Shield:

Winners in 1912.
Losers in 1928, 1994 and 1995.

Full Members Cup:

Winners in 1987 when a goal from Colin Hendry proved enough against Charlton at Wembley.

Right:
Party Mood...
Alan 'Birdy' Birkbeck celebrates with fellow Rovers fans during the Premiership party at Ewood

30 Joe Clennell signed for Rovers from which club in April 1911?
(Blackpool)

31 In April 1912, who did Rovers beat 4-1 to clinch the championship?
(West Brom)

Family Stories

Ask your Dad...football in ye olden days was a different ball game.
So too, for that matter, were the players.

Family Stories

Ronnie Clayton

Rovers legend Ronnie Clayton remembers one incident on a freezing cold Ewood Park pitch which these days would probably spark legal action and writs, let alone a good old scrap.

Right:
Official Ronnie Clayton Testimonial match programme

Far Right:
Ronnie Clayton in action

"It was a home game against Preston and must have been about November because the pitch was frozen and they hadn't rolled it so it was full of ruts," says Ronnie.

"I went in for a tackle on Tom Finney, who was my hero when I used to play junior football in Preston, and he slid on the frozen turf for about ten yards.

"When he got up his body was covered in blood from the ruts. He got up, squared up to me and said: "Fizzin' heck Ron!" and got on with the game. Simple as that.

"People say it's a dirty game today, but in those days it just wasn't as big an issue. If you kicked out you didn't bother about it - because you knew that it would be your turn next."

Ronnie Clayton made his first senior appearance for Rovers in 1951, his last almost two decades later in 1969.

For nearly 20 years Ronnie pulled on the blue and white, notching up 665 appearances, playing his way into Ewood Park legend status.

Thank heavens then for Preston North End...as Ronnie explains: "I played in and around Preston as a youngster, and when I was 14 North End wanted to take a look at my 16-year-old brother Ken. My father said if they wanted Ken then they had to take me too...they told me to come back in two years!

"Three weeks later we both played a trial at Ewood Park and were signed by Rovers the same night. I made my first team debut at the age of 16, kept my place and was made captain within weeks of coming back from two years national service at the age of 20."

And the rest, as they say, is history. Every diehard supporter knows the Ronnie Clayton story, how he went on to dominate the game for both Rovers and England... and yet he is still one of the most approachable people in the game and has never courted public adoration.

Right:
Ronnie Clayton scoring against Liverpool in 1958

Below:
Ronnie Clayton pictured at Ewood Park before the start of his testimonial match

He got it mind you, but it was never a burden. It still isn't today - he's what you would call a people person.

"In the 1950s nobody had a car so the players and their families all lived near the ground, near each other. It was a wonderful atmosphere and it helped a great deal on the pitch too. It was like one big family, and that was the way of things at all the clubs.

"I have always made it my way to meet with the public and I still get involved in presentations and such like. As a player I gave 100% and I think the fans recognised that, so we were invariably on very good terms. Back then, all the players mixed with the supporters, often as their next-door neighbours, whereas now they seem far more distant.

"To me it was a golden era and I was proud to be playing...we even used to stay on to do extra work at training sessions! I loved playing and I loved training.

"Squad players got almost double the wage of fringe players, and there was always someone waiting to step into your boots."

Even for legends.

"There were a lot of great players, and if one got injured there was always at least one player to come straight in. Stanley Matthews told me that when he was at Stoke there were five very good outside rights, and if he had two bad games that would be it, and he was the greatest. It was the same at Ewood Park.

32 In what year did Bob Crompton resign as honorary manager of the club?
(1931)

33 Which Rovers striker scored 35 goals in 39 league games in 1926-27?
(Ted Harper)

Left:
Ronnie Clayton today

"It meant a lot, not just in terms of the game, because you'd only get £8 a week if you weren't in the team, the same as you were paid in the close season.

"I remember Tommy Docherty complaining to the Preston manager about the close season cuts, that it was unfair he had to take a pay cut when Tom Finney didn't. "Aye, but you're not Tom Finney," his boss said.

"But I play just as well in the summer," he replied.

"We were on £15 a week, plus £2 for a win and £1 for a draw. There was no point moving to another club because the wages were standardised nationally.

"A lot of clubs were after me when I was about 24 - Chelsea, Manchester City, Manchester United, Wolves, Liverpool - but there was never any question of leaving. I loved it at Ewood and besides, there was nothing to be gained financially and I didn't want to uproot."

In fact Ronnie has remained in the same part of the world since 1961 when he sold his business and settled in the Ribble Valley.

"I moved to Wilpshire 37 years ago and have stayed there ever since. Previously I ran a small newsagent in Darwen, until Rovers asked me to get rid of it!

"In retrospect they were right to do so. I was up at 4.30am and we wouldn't close until 7pm, so it was a long day, and it did start to affect the football. In fact I think now that that might have had something to do with me losing my place in the England team. When the photographers used to come round to do the team photos I'd be nodding off!

"It was a real shame for me personally because playing for your country is a real honour, but playing alongside legends like Finney, Matthews and Duncan Edwards was a special treat. I still see a lot of the old players which is nice.

Now an Ewood Park tour guide Ronnie is just proud to be back on the staff: "I love doing the tours. I get a real buzz telling the old stories and answering questions about the old days."

34 Who did Rovers beat in the 1928 FA Cup final?
(Huddersfield Town)

35 Who scored twice for Rovers in the 1928 FA Cup final?
(Jack Roscamp)

Below Left:
A young Bryan Douglas

Right:
Bryan Douglas, collectors' cigarette card

Family Stories
Bryan Douglas

Bryan Douglas is guaranteed a permanent place in Ewood Park's Hall of Fame.

For 14 seasons twinkle-toed Duggie teased and tormented defenders with his wing wizardry to the delight of an adoring public.

With top side of 400 appearances and more than 100 goals he assumed legendary status. Bryan Douglas was a true football great.

But his love affair with Rovers goes deeper than that, far deeper.

The fact that he played for Rovers so well and for so long is almost incidental...for Bryan will always consider himself a fan first and a player second.

Still living in Darwen, his love for the club, which first blossomed some six decades back, remains as passionate as ever.

"This is my town. I was born and brought up in Blackburn so Rovers have always been my team. They were my one and only club and to have been paid to do something that I would have done for nothing was wonderful, absolutely wonderful."

"We were paid £20 a week - everyone was, whether you were Stanley Matthews or Joe Bloggs. I thought it was a good wage, far better than the average man in the street and, irrespective of what anyone might say, footballers lived quite comfortably."

Twenty pounds...it would only just about cover an afternoon watching football these days!

But it was still a good deal more than Bryan had been used to. Before finding international stardom as a footballer, he had worked as a motor engineer at Intack, a job his father introduced him to "to pay his dues."

Four years later he was pulling on an England shirt.

But let's go even further back: "Having played for my school and for the town team I was pencilled in for a trial with Rovers - along with a heck of a lot of other lads. I made the next stage and was asked to train on Tuesday and Thursday nights along with about 50 others - part time pros, trialists and the like.

"It was around then I joined the ground staff at Ewood Park. When I left school my father insisted I got a job, but I started taking so much time off to go training and play games that I was given an ultimatum.

"It was decision time but really there was no decision to be made. There was only one winner. I learned to clean boots, wash and sweep the dressing rooms and terracing...character building stuff.

Left:
Bryan Douglas in great form after 15 minutes, Rovers v Spurs

Below:
This autographed drawing of Bryan Douglas by LET artist Jack Tipping incorporated 4200 ink dots, each one put on with the point of a pen

Facing Page Right:
Bryan Douglas' testimonial match programme 1969

Facing Page Bottom Right:
Bryan Douglas today

Facing Page Far Right:
Douglas in action in the Rovers v Wednesday match 1963

"Actually, it made it easier when I broke through into the team because I knew all the players..."

Bryan finally got his big break in 1955, plunged straight into one of the most experienced and talented sides in Rovers history. The young starry-eyed lad made his full bow on the right wing at Notts County on 5th September 1954 alongside the likes of Tommy Briggs, Eddie Quigley and Bobby Langton - all of them 10 or 15 years older. For Bryan it was like serving an apprenticeship.

It was to be his one and only appearance, but the following season he became established. And how...playing 90 games on the bounce.

So what was it like to be a Rovers star in the 50s?

"On match days we would make our own way to the ground for about an hour before kick off. I used to play snooker in Blackburn with some friends in the morning and then catch the bus to the game. I remember listening in to the supporters going to the game - I could get away with listening in early on as I wasn't recognised!

"When I became more well known - famous if you like - I made sure I never lost touch with the people I had grown up with. I went out of my way to talk to them all - still do. I didn't want anyone to ever say I changed because I had "made it."

"It is much harder for players now because they are made into megastars, but even in my day you had to watch where you went and what you did. Your moves were closely monitored and you had to watch your behaviour.

"Today's players are recognised wherever they go - not just in the town where they play. That is all down to the media, particularly the national newspapers and television.

"For me it was more a local thing, even when I was playing for England. You were recognised in London only if it was a match day and you were in and around Wembley. In fact I used to get off the coach before we arrived so I could meet friends and relatives without being swamped!"

Times have certainly changed and Bryan is the first to admit it. Take Brockhall, for example, as far removed from the 1950s training schedule as it is possible to get.

"Training? It was pretty basic stuff. Whether you were 6'2" and weighed 15 stone or 5'2" and weighed 9 stone we used to do the same thing, on the cinders at the back of the Blackburn End.

"We'd warm up, move on to quicker stuff and then play 6/7 a-side...we used to do sprinting too, but only on Fridays! We called it "quick work"...it was an easy morning because we used to finish at 11am.

36 Who was Rovers captain in the 1928 FA Cup final?
(Harry Healless)

37 Eddie Crossan made his Rovers debut in a 4-3 win over Sunderland at Ewood Park in January of which year?
(1948)

"Then we would be told the team for the Saturday. They would pin a sheet on the wall and you knew exactly who would be playing because there were no subs - just the starting 11 and the reserve.

"Tracksuits hadn't even been invented at that time! We were issued with kit at the beginning of every season comprising of spikes (running shoes), pumps, socks, a woolly sweater, a vest and some shorts and they did you for the season. By July all the equipment was dirty, darned and patched up.

"It was a different game. Today I think it's much harder for players to stay at one club like I did. Agents negotiate deals which are difficult, even impossible, for players to refuse...we never had anything like that.

"I did become unsettled once in the early 60s and I put in for a transfer. I had dug a bit of a hole for myself and the team was struggling. I thought I was getting a bit stale and I found myself going through the motions a bit. So I decided it was time to move on.

"The manager told me in no uncertain terms that leaving wasn't an option. You have to remember that all footballers were on one-year contracts and at the end of the year you couldn't leave of your own free will.

"Either the club retained you or put you on the transfer list - if they wanted a fee they had to pay your wages, if you were on a free you were effectively sacked. So if they wanted a fee you couldn't leave. I stayed."

Just as well for us...Bryan's bid came on the back of the 1960 FA Cup Final defeat at Wembley against Wolves.

"I remember the 1960 Final vividly. I felt sorry for myself and for the team, but most of all I felt sorry for the thousands of supporters. It was the biggest disappointment of my life and to this day I still feel it.

"I know what a supporter feels because first and foremost I am a supporter. I've followed the Rovers since I was a kid and it hurts me just as much as it does everyone else when results go badly.

"But, even after a heavy defeat or a big disappointment, I still bounce back full of optimism for the next match. Always will."

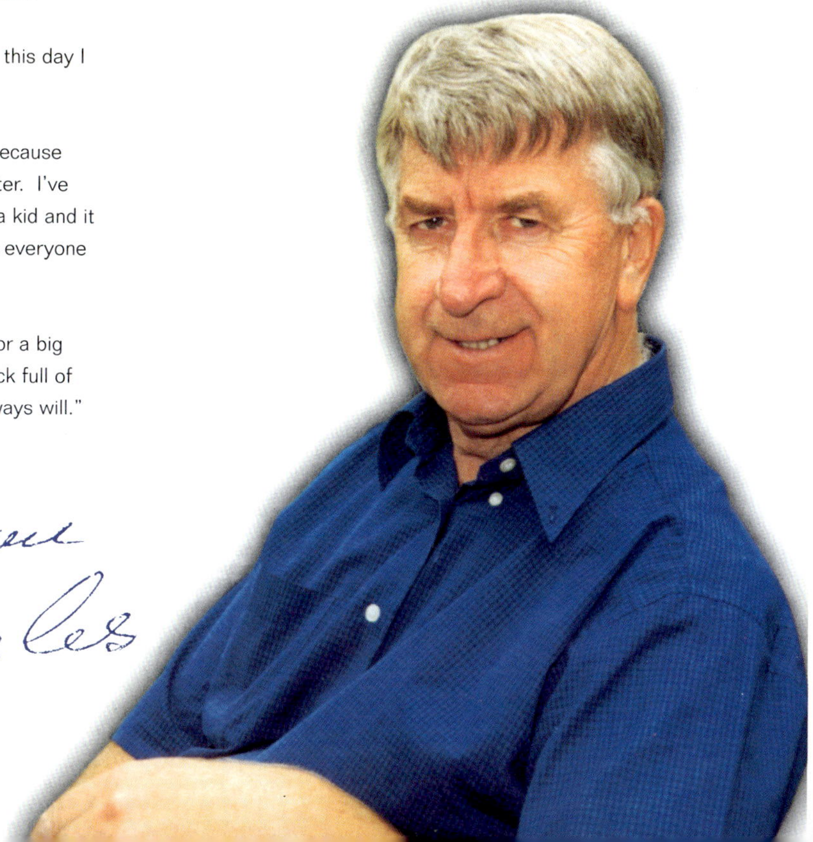

38 Who was Rovers top scorer and the only player to reach double figures in both the 1948/49 and 1949/50 campaigns - his only two seasons for the club?

(Dennis Westcott)

Family Stories

Harry Healless' 1928 Cup Final Victory

Top Right:
Two collectors' cigarette cards featuring Harry Healless

Right:
Harry Healless' birth certificate

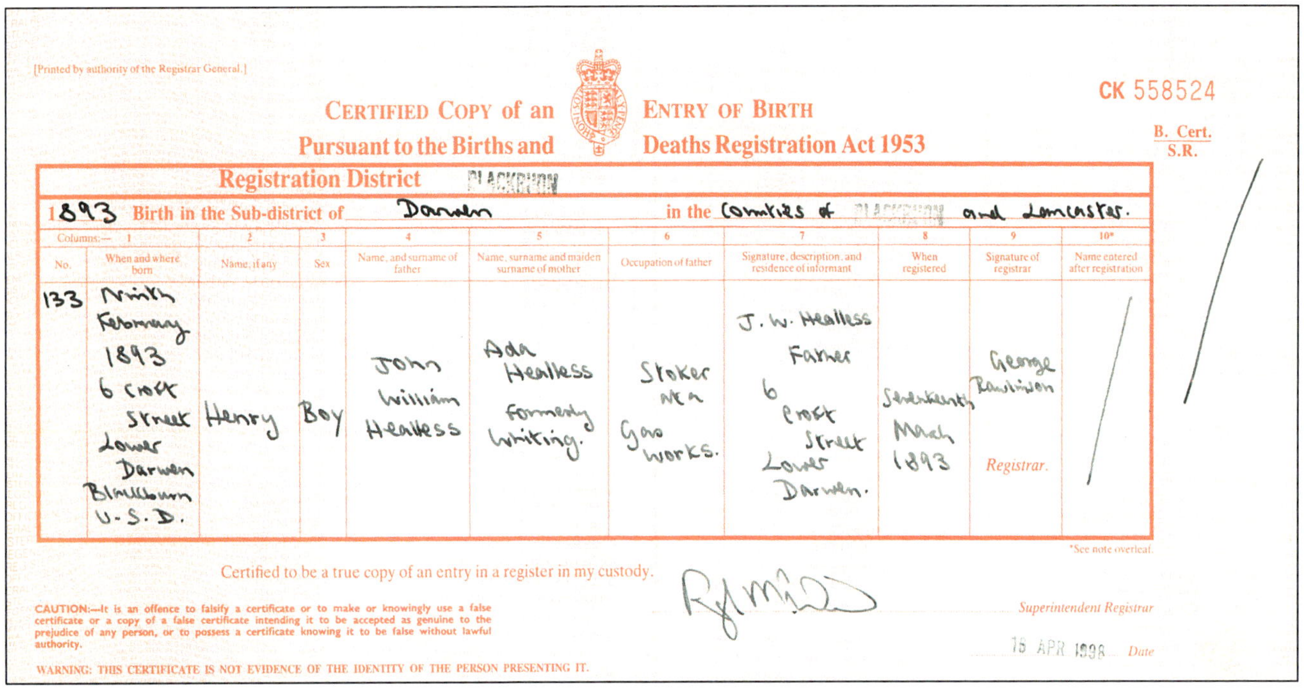

[Printed by authority of the Registrar General.]

CERTIFIED COPY of an ENTRY OF BIRTH
Pursuant to the Births and Deaths Registration Act 1953

CK 558524

B. Cert. S.R.

Registration District BLACKBURN

1893 Birth in the Sub-district of Darwen in the Counties of BLACKBURN and Lancaster.

No.	When and where born	Name, if any	Sex	Name, and surname of father	Name, surname and maiden surname of mother	Occupation of father	Signature, description, and residence of informant	When registered	Signature of registrar	Name entered after registration
133	Ninth February 1893 6 Croft Street Lower Darwen Blackburn U.S.D.	Henry	Boy	John William Healless	Ada Healless formerly Whiting.	Stoker at a Gas works.	J. W. Healless Father 6 Croft Street Lower Darwen.	Seventeenth March 1893	George Rawlinson Registrar.	

*See note overleaf.

Certified to be a true copy of an entry in a register in my custody.

Superintendent Registrar

15 APR 1998 Date

CAUTION:—It is an offence to falsify a certificate or to make or knowingly use a false certificate or a copy of a false certificate intending it to be accepted as genuine to the prejudice of any person, or to possess a certificate knowing it to be false without lawful authority.

WARNING: THIS CERTIFICATE IS NOT EVIDENCE OF THE IDENTITY OF THE PERSON PRESENTING IT.

39 Who was the first Rover to score a goal under manager Jackie Bestall?

(John Wharton)

40 How many goals did top scorer Ted Harper bag in 40 league and cup games for Rovers during the 1925/26 season?

(Ted Harper scored 43 goals, the highest league scorer for the 1925/26 season)

41 Who scored a hat-trick when Rovers dealt neighbouring Burnley an 8-3 hammering at Ewood Park in November 1929?

(Arthur Groves)

The story of Harry Healless warms the heart of every true Blue and White stalwart, for it's a tale of a local lad made good.....very good.

Born within kicking distance of the ground, he made his Rovers bow in a 2-0 defeat at Sheffield United in October 1919.

But defeat didn't deter the young half-back's enthusiasm and Harry went on to wear the Ewood number 4 (or sometimes number 5) shirt close-on 400 times.

He made two appearances for England and even went on to coach the Rovers A team and later the seniors.

But an impressive appearance record and a couple of caps were far from the pinnacle of his career at his beloved hometown club.

For Harry went on to skipper Bob Crompton's Ewood side to lift the FA Cup after a resounding 3-1 Wembley win over Huddersfield Town.

Left:
Blackburn Rovers celebratory dinner menu

Below Left:
Geoff Hindle

Right:
Harry Healless at the wheel of the tractor with a few of the Blackburn Rovers players during a break in their training at Cleveleys

Above:
Old collectors' card

Below:
The commemorative plaque at No 6 Top o'th Croft, Ewood

Such is the romantic appeal of Harry's tale that one Blackburn couple have dedicated their lives to keeping his memory alive.

In the mid seventies Geoff and Lynn Hindle moved into number 6 Top o'th Croft, Ewood and shortly after discovered that it had been the birthplace of the unforgettable Rovers captain over three quarters of a century previous.

Lynn became interested in the history of the row of cottages, situated only a couple of hundred yards from the Darwen End stand.

She did a little research at the town's library but it took husband Geoff - a lifelong Rovers fan - a couple of years to make the connection between the name on the rent book and the former Ewood skipper.

"As soon as we thought there might be a link between the house and one of the club's most memorable players we both stepped up the search for evidence." says Geoff.

"We managed to acquire a copy of his birth certificate which stated that he was actually born in the cottage.

"Then we decided to collect artifacts relating to Harry and his life as a Rover. We now have programmes, cigarette cards, newspapers - it's quite a collection."

So comprehensive is the Hindle's treasure trove that they have newspapers from the day of that memorable FA Cup final victory, a mint condition Wembley programme as well as autographs and two genuine ticket stubs.

"Harry was the only Blackburn-born player in the 1928 Cup Final winning team and we think it's imperative that his memory lives on.

"We were so keen to get some form of recognition for Harry that we approached Blackburn Civic Society and after some deliberation they erected a plaque outside our home to commemorate his birthplace."

Programme
F.A. CUP FINAL
Played at Wembley Stadium
HUDDERSFIELD TOWN
v.
BLACKBURN ROVERS
Saturday, April 21st, 1928
KICK-OFF 3.0 p.m.

Above:
1928 FA Cup Final programme

Centre:
Harry Healless with daughter Ada

Right:
Illustration by B. Villiers, part of Geoff and Lynn Hindle's extensive BRFC collection

The Hindles are extremely proud of their collection and in particular the plaque which is a source of much interest from fellow Rovers fanatics, especially on matchdays.

"Every Saturday afternoon we are swamped with people admiring the plaque and taking photographs. We always welcome people in to view our collection of Harry Healless artifacts. It's great to see other fans getting the same enjoyment the collection gives us."

42 Who was the only man not to miss a league or cup game in the 1930-31 season?

(Goalkeeper Cliff Binns)

Family Stories

Stuart Metcalfe

These days Stuart Metcalfe is just as well known for his pedigree Afghan hounds as for his terrier like midfield presence as a 1970s Rovers' workhorse.

But back then, Metcalfe - a deceptively frail figure - played over 425 games for Rovers over 14 seasons and fast earned a reputation as a no-nonsense, tough-tackling and competitive midfielder...with a quick temper.

His most infamous moment came as a direct result of the red mist and is forever immortalised in Rovers' folklore as the day Ian St John got smacked.

"I was always bad tempered, even in school games," says Stuart, now a mental health nurse at Calderstones Hospital.

"I'm not saying I was the best player in the world but to me every player - especially in midfield - needs a bit of aggression.

"Some of my bookings were stupid - if someone kicked me, instead of walking away I'd go up and hit 'em. The opposition manager used to work it into their tactics: "Go and wind Metcalfe up, we'll have him sent off."

"I remember playing at Tranmere one Friday night. Ian St John kicked me in the mouth and knocked two teeth out so I got up and lamped him one. I got sent off, but that's what it was like.

"In those days referees actually let a lot more slide and today I couldn't afford to play like that. I'd never get a game, I'd always be suspended...but I still think you need that bit of aggression."

In the end Stuart reckons that boss Gordon Lee helped him curb a lot of that aggression - by keeping him on the bench!

Stuart left Rovers behind in 1980, moving over the water for a stint in US soccer when fate intervened and at 32 years old he returned to Ewood Park. Walking his Afghans - originally a gift from Rovers team-mate John Kenyon - through Pleasington Park the statuesque animals took off and ripped through the middle of a Rovers training session. And it was former midfield partner Tony Parkes, with whom he played over 300 games, who persuaded him to return.

Right: A young Stuart Metcalfe in action

43 How many times did Bobby Langton play for England whilst on the books at Ewood?

(Seven)

44 In April 1937, Rovers put nine goals past Nottingham Forest but how many did Forest pull back?

(one)

45 Rovers sold inside right Syd Puddefoot to his hometown club in February 1932 - which club was that?

(West Ham)

Above: A young Stuart Metcalfe

Right: Phillips of Bolton comes across to challenge Stuart Metcalfe at Ewood Park

"I spent 15 months playing for Baltimore but I was at a loose end when I came back. Parkesy asked what I was doing and if I was interested in coaching the reserves on a non-contract basis. I played just one game towards the end of the season when Noel Brotherston was taken ill. The squad wasn't very big in the early 80s, but still I assumed I'd only be sub. It turned out I was on from the whistle - I was fit and I didn't do myself an injustice - I did score that own goal which lost us the game, but still..."

Blackburn-born Stuart who went to the same primary school as Fred Pickering, made his debut in 1968, aged 17 and sporting a crew cut.

But as the hairstyles changed as the 70s kicked in, so did football - and Blackburn Rovers suffered more than most.

"I had a crew cut when I started in the first team - Jimmy Gordon (first team coach) saw to that. I had long hair even in the 60s, and every day Jimmy would say "If you don't get your hair cut Metcalfe you're not training!" and he would make me clean the changing room with a tooth brush and train on my own later.

"One morning I went in the changing room and the door locked behind me, four of them jumped me, put me on the medical table and slashed my hair all over the place with scissors. It was a right mess and I had to get a bloody crew cut! Jimmy Gordon was very strict, a really hard disciplinarian. You couldn't mess about with Jimmy but he was a very good trainer.

"At first I was being groomed as a replacement for Bryan Douglas on the wing, and when Mike Ferguson left I got my chance - Rovers had to sell players then in order to balance the books and after relegation from Division One in 1966 a lot of star names moved on.

"I was only about 17, but even then there were a lot of good pros behind me to tell me where I was going wrong, people like Keith Newton, Ronnie Clayton and Duggie, who I always tried to model my game on.

"Throughout the 1970s there wasn't much stability in the team - I'd lose count of the number of managers and centre forwards we had coming through Ewood Park."

Stuart, along with Tony Parkes and Derek Fazackerley, remained loyal to the club throughout.

"If Liverpool or someone had come in for me when I was 21 I would have gone because I would have liked to play in a higher league. I joined in 1966 when we'd just been relegated from the old First Division and the highest I ever played in was the second.

"I don't regret staying at Blackburn, not at all, and I had some fantastic times - the promotion season from Division Three will always be the highlight of my career.

"If I was playing now I probably wouldn't get a game in Rovers first team...I would be a fringe player at best. Then it wasn't a squad game, we made do with what we had!

"Tony and I played so many games together we had a good understanding and I think the fans always appreciated that we always gave it 100%. It helps if you're winning of course, but supporters aren't mugs and they will always support someone who works hard for the club - people like Parkesey and Faz. The money wasn't a consideration then - you were lucky to get a £10 rise year on year - because you were playing for Blackburn, you were playing for the club and for the supporters.

"We had a rota at the club for players to make personal appearances in pubs and clubs and so on, very regular, once or twice a week.

"To me that's what it's all about, especially as a local lad. We'd always meet up with the supporters at the old Ewood Club and have a few beers. You'd get stick if you had had a bad game, but you accept it. At the end of the day it's the supporters that pay your wages.

"I can even remember Jack Walker, who wasn't the multi-millionaire he is today, coming into the changing room to chat with the players as far back as the late 60s."

"My dad used to take me on Ewood when I was a nipper...Jack Campbell actually discovered me when I was about 10 and I played on Ewood for St Peters in the Jubilee Shield. It was always a treat for the kids to play on Ewood, and we won 4-1. I scored two goals which I will never forget.

"Jack Campbell came round to the house after the game to have a word with my Mum and asked me to come down to train.

"I was made an apprentice when I was 14 which was a dream come true.

"You look at the ground now and you forget what it was like when I was playing, even small things like the changing rooms. It's a beautiful ground, absolutely marvellous".

Right:
Stuart Metcalfe today with one of his beloved Afghan hounds

46 How much did Rovers shell out to land Bobby Langton in the late 1930s - £20, £30 or £50
(£50)

47 How many consecutive league games did Walter Crook start to set a new Football League record?
(208)

Family Stories

The Godfather - Tony Parkes

Below:
Tony Parkes in action

Right:
Tony Parkes in full flight

Tony Parkes, who entered the 21st century as the club's 25th Manager, actually took a drop in pay to join Rovers.

Non-league Buxton Town benefited to the tune of a princely £3,000 when he signed on the dotted line at Ewood Park close on 30 years ago.

Have Rovers ever conducted a better bit of business? Talk about value for money!

Tony Parkes is top of the league when it comes to outstanding and unbroken service. No-one can match him. Player, coach, manager, whatever his role, Sheffield-born Tony has always been a true son of BRFC.

"I maybe a Yorkshireman, but I consider myself a Blackburnian. This will always be the place I look upon as home."

It may have been the dawn of the 70s when he arrived as a wide-eyed 20-year-old hoping for a break into the big-time but he remembers it like yesterday.
"My recollections are vivid, from walking up Nuttall Street on my way to a trial game, to calling in at the commercial office (portakabin!) to ask where I should go, to meeting Eddie Quigley in the dressing room, to playing against Leeds reserves.

"John Connelly was playing for us that night too and I must have done okay for they invited me to play in another trial against Manchester United. After that they made me an offer to sign on £25-a week. I was earning £30-a-week as a wall and floor tiler and picking up an extra £7-a-game playing for Buxton...but it was still a no choice situation.

"I couldn't wait to sign and, really, the money wasn't a consideration. It was just something I knew I had to do."

Tony, a striker back in those days with a better than a goal-a-game record to his name, stayed in club digs over the Fox and Hounds pub near the ground.

"Mr and Mrs Bremner ran it and I used to help out in the pub, often serving behind the bar - one of our best customers was Don Martin, then a real crowd favourite with Rovers' fans. I think the management turned a blind eye to his drinking, it certainly didn't seem to hamper him as a footballer!"

Nor did smoking have much of an adverse effect on the likes of Simon Garner either....one of the stars from the Parkes' 30-year scrapbook.

48 From which club did Rovers buy Jack Roscamp in 1922?
(Wallsend)

49 Who replaced Bob Crompton as Rovers manager in January 1946?
(Eddie Hapgood)

"Great finisher, had he played for the club a decade later he could have become a huge star. I always felt Stuart Metcalfe was in that sort of category too, then there were the likes of David Wagstaffe, who could hit a pass yards from one pace, Howard Kendall, a top quality midfielder - those were the sort of players I admired prior to the dawn of our Premiership era.

"Winning the Premiership must rank as Rovers finest hour in my time here but my proudest moment was when I was given the opportunity to lead the team out at Wembley for the play-off final with Leicester. That was special, so special and I was deeply moved by the whole experience my most emotional day in football.

"The day we clinched the Premiership at Anfield was marvellous and I can remember every minute of it not just the game but the build up and the celebrations.

"All the people crammed into Anfield seemed to want us to win, in order to deny Manchester United. When Jamie Redknapp scored to put Liverpool ahead near the end everything threatened to go sour, but the cameramen situated next to our dug out shouted across that it didn't matter for United had only managed a draw and the title was ours.

"Kenny and Ray were dancing on the pitch and we were all joining in...it must have looked very strange for our game was still going on. When we got back into the dressing room everyone was so happy. Kenny hadn't allowed any talk of winning the league right up to the final day and so we hadn't been able to make any plans in advance.

"We decided to try to gatecrash the Bistro French restaurant in Preston and the owner Ian Boasman welcomed us with open arms. The place looked full when we got there but somehow they managed to squeeze us in. The Drifters were on and it was quite a night, I will never forget it that's for sure."

Other major memories?

"It is difficult as there are so many but the time when we came back from being two down to beat Plymouth 5-2 at Ewood, travelling on the first trip aboard the League Liner special train, going 3-0 up and then hanging on one Boxing Day at Burnley and scoring a couple when we hit Oldham for six.

50 Only two players "top scored" for Rovers in an eight-year spell between 1953 and 1961 - Tommy Briggs was one, who was the other?
(Peter Dobing)

51 Was ex-Rovers full back Dave Whelan born in Bradford or Wigan?
(Bradford)

"I will always look back with affection of that great year under Gordon Lee when we took the Third Division title in 1975.
It was a real team effort, Gordon wouldn't have had it any other way, and we all seemed to mate around together in a group, wives and all.

"We did an awful lot of personal appearances back then.... I thoroughly enjoyed it, pushing over piles of pennies in pubs and clubs for charity and all that sort of stuff. People would talk football to you all night and why not? Rovers is their club after all and players have a responsibility to communicate with the fans."

Tony's golden memories don't all revolve around a particular season, game, goal or individual....there are others.

"Some very unusual things have happened which no-one outside the club has ever seen or got to know about.

Left:
Tony Parkes today

"A couple of them involved our former manager Bobby Saxton. Bob used to go down to Pleasington, where we trained back then, to make sure everything was okay before the lads arrived.

"One day there was a car parked on the pitch and the windows where all steamed up...Bob went along in his normal straightforward style and knocked on the window. Through the steam he could see there was let's say a courting couple inside....he said they had better hurry up as 25 lads were due to arrive any minute!

"Bob had another experience with a steamed up car a few weeks later but this time the finding was most disturbing....the chap inside the car had committed suicide.

"Everything seemed to happen to Bob down at Pleasington - one time the ball went into the river and he decided to wade in and get it. It was mid-winter and the current was strong, much stronger than he had thought. Within seconds he was being swept away and in no time at all he had travelled about 150 yards. Luckily, as we ran down the river in pursuit, he was able to grab hold of a boulder and eventually force himself on to the bank. He was very shocked by it all and needed a good few minutes to get his composure back. Eventually he groaned that he had been through all of that and still hadn't retrieved the ball...at which point Paul Comstive jumped in and got it!"

Tony admits that on signing he had little idea the association would span three decades: "Blimey I was hardly looking further than the end of the season back then; never would I have envisaged all this.

"Blackburn Rovers has played a major part in my life and I hope it continues to do so. To be manager is a great personal honour for me and who knows how many memories lie ahead."

BRINDLE ANTIQUES & FINE ARTS

MEMBERS OF LAPADA

Fine Oil Painting by William Mellor

A family run business of almost 40 years experience, located in the heart of the Ribble Valley.

Stockists of fine furniture, Paintings, China, Bronzes, Silverware.

A professional expert advice & guidance on the purchase of quality Antique furniture & decorative items from Billiard rooms to Ballrooms.

Tel:01200 440025
E-Mail: tbrindle@globalnet.co.uk

Fax:01200 440090
http://www.antiqueweb.co.uk/tbrindle/

4 SAWLEY ROAD ● CHATBURN ● CLITHEROE ● LANCS ● BB7 4AS

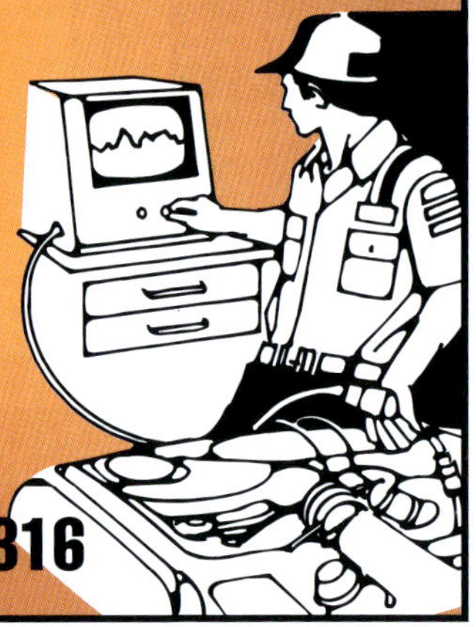

Family Stories

Fred Pickering

Dateline: Boxing Day 1963
Venue: Upton Park
Scoreline: West Ham United 2, Rovers 8

"Our dressing room was buzzing afterwards. To say the mood was upbeat would be putting it mildly. Everyone was elated, particularly Andy McEvoy and myself - we had both scored hat-tricks. But Jimmy Gordon, our trainer, was soon to change the atmosphere. Jimmy, who was forever clutching a pad and a pen, recording statistics, relayed to us the match facts. He claimed that West Ham had recorded 20 shots and scored twice while we had recorded 10 in scoring eight times.

"We thought that was a feather in our caps, but Jimmy stunned us by stating that he felt something was wrong with our performance - basically we hadn't created enough chances!"

Fred Pickering still carries a look of disbelief when he recalls that incident after what still ranks as one of the club's most memorable away results.

But, there's more....

"We had travelled down on Christmas Day lunchtime from Preston Station, arriving at our hotel in Green Park to find the place deserted, apart from the manager, a porter and a couple of staff. Evening meals clearly weren't on the menu so we had to send out for fish and chips!

"We just about managed tea and toast the following morning before a cross city coach trip to the ground. We were still fairly bleary-eyed - and hungry - for what was a morning kick-off....God alone knows what we might have done to them if we had been wide awake!"

That performance, coupled with a 7-2 home success over the mighty Spurs (Danny Blanchflower, Dave Mackay et al) three months before, will always remain the highlights of Fred's senior career at Ewood Park. But it was a junior success that really first catapulted him into the public eye when he skippered the Rovers youngsters to a wonderful FA Youth Cup triumph....over West Ham.

Fred is a true and proud Blackburnian. Now approaching his 59th birthday (January 2000) he still lives in the Mill Hill district where he was born and raised. As a pupil at St Peter's RC Junior School his soccer prowess got him into the school team three years ahead of schedule.

Left:
A young Fred Pickering emerges from the tunnel

"We were short of players and the football teacher, Miss Shepherd, asked for volunteers. I was only nine but that wasn't going to stoe. I would have done more or less anything for a game of football."

52 How much did Rovers pay Burnley for John "Jack" Bruton in December 1929 - was it £65, £650 or £6,500?
(£6,500)

53 Which London club did Rovers dump out in the semi final of the 1928 FA Cup before lifting the trophy at Wembley?
(Arsenal)

On leaving formal education at 15 he took an engineering job at the Northrop factory and played, by invitation, for the Rovers colts. He took an apprenticeship just three months before being issued with a professional contract.

"I went from earning £2-a-week at the Northrop to £5 on the ground staff to £7 as a pro in a matter of weeks. I thought all my birthdays had come at once."

A self-confessed Rovers fanatic, only missing games through either playing commitments or a lack of cash, Fred had found heaven. Playing the game he loved for a living for his home-town club.

Left:
Elegant Pickering on the ball

Right:
Fred pickering today

"Those were great days. I was particularly pally with Mike England who came through the ranks with me - as did Keith Newton. We were all part of that youth team and all got to the top of the tree. Mind you, one or two of the West Ham lads didn't do too badly either, Bobby Moore, Geoff Hurst and Martin Peters! Mike and I established ourselves in the first team at the same time - we were both playing full back. My debut was at Leicester in the October of 1959. We won 3-2 and I also played against Burnley and West Brom that season, both home games which ended up winning 3-2 funnily enough."

Fred had a bit of a run the following season before his career took a real twist.

"I was back in the reserves and we had a few injuries prior to a game at Preston. Jackie Campbell, who ran the team with Eric Bell, asked me if I fancied having a go up front. I said no problem and played well, scoring twice at Deepdale.

"Derek Dougan, who was our first choice team striker had been over to Belgium talking over a possible transfer and he didn't get back until late on the Friday night before a First Division game against Manchester City at Ewood.

"Jack Marshall decided to leave Dougan out and picked me instead - as an out-and-out striker. I was nervous, even though Dougan had wished me all the best just before the game, but as soon as I got going I loved it."

Fred scored twice as City were crushed 4-1 and English football suddenly had a new centre forward to talk about. He averaged a goal every other game for the remainder of the season. But his most impressive season came in 1963-64 when he forged a telepathic partnership with McEvoy.

Rovers played some scintillating soccer and, in all competitions, their twin strike force shared an astonishing 62 goals, Pickering with 26 and McEvoy with 36.

54 Welsh striker of the 50s who also made a huge impact on Merseyside. Name him
(Roy Vernon)

55 Striker Andy McEvoy came over to Ewood Park from which fair city?
(Dublin)

56 Who am I? I won 44 caps for Wales, played at the heart of defence and moved onto London before returning to my homeland. Also had a business in East Lancashire
(Mike England)

In March 1964 Fred upped sticks and left - why?

"It was all about money I suppose. I had got in with the England squad and I felt I was deserving of a rise. You looked after your own contract negotiations then and I remember going in and asking for a £10-per-week rise from £25 to £35.

"The request was refused and I said I would be better looking for someone who would meet the price. Next news Rovers had announced that they wanted £90,000 for me and Everton came in.

"I got the £35-a-week and a better bonus structure so off I went without too much thought to be honest. It all happened in a couple of crazy days."

It proved a good move for Fred who quickly found himself more and more in the spotlight. Selected for an England trip to Ireland and America he was handed his international bow by Alf Ramsey.

"We were playing the States, who included players of all nationalities, and Alf was very nervous of the fixture considering it was a friendly. He still harboured memories of being part of the team that had lost that time to America during the World Cup in Brazil in 1950."

Ramsey needn't have lost any sleep - England, inspired by Pickering's hat-trick, won 10-0. Surprisingly, Fred's international career never really took off, he played only twice more and no-one, especially the man himself, has ever been able to work out what went wrong.

"I got a knee injury soon after joining Everton and it held me back. The cartilage kept popping out and the medical people of the time were very wary about touching it. And I did have a heated conversation with Alf once, about him playing me in a role I wasn't comfortable with, but it can hardly explain what happened. One minute I was a hero and the next I wasn't even picked.

"The dodgy knee not only cost me a place in the World Cup squad in 1966, it also meant I missed out on the FA Cup Final against Sheffield Wednesday.

Fred moved to Birmingham for £50,000 in 1967: "Great club, loved it down there, such a friendly atmosphere - but the family couldn't settle and we moved back north to Blackpool.

"Eventually my knee started to worsen and I was on the point of announcing my retirement at Blackpool at 31 when suddenly the chance came to re-join Rovers. It was the early 70s and the club was in a right state. I managed a couple of goals but decided to call it a day after Ken Furphy arrived."

Since then Fred's interest in Rovers and football has always been from a distance: "I was never a good spectator and going to watch matches holds little appeal for me. I had a great time as a player, nothing could ever compare to that, and those memories will do me very nicely thank you."

Family Stories

Rovers' Gallery

Colin Hendry

Edward Colin James Hendry arrived at Ewood Park in time to score the winning goal in the 1987 Full Members Cup Final, becoming an instant hero with the fans.

Dubbed Mr Blackburn Rovers, Hendry would never think twice about risking life and limb for the cause, often throwing his head in where most defenders would be wary of putting in a boot.

Left for Manchester City before returning under Kenny Dalglish to play a major role in the 1995 Premiership title success.

Captained Scotland on several occasions and played in the 1998 World Cup in France.

Bob Crompton

Full-back Bob Crompton made 576 appearances in a Rovers shirt before becoming a director of the club. In 1926 he took on the position of manager, winning the FA Cup in 1928.

It is a fitting tribute that after Crompton's departure Rovers were relegated, and in his first full season back in charge he won promotion back into the First Division!

Rated by many as the greatest all-round Rover of them all.

57. Against whom did Mike Ferguson score his famous solo wonder goal

(Aston Villa)

58. What job did Bill Eckersley have prior to joining Rovers?

(A lorry driver)

59. What was the name of the brother of a famous Rovers' skipper, who broke his leg in April 1957 at Middlesbrough?

(Ken Clayton)

Derek Fazackerley

Derek Fazackerley holds the club record for the most appearances with an astonishing 674 games for Rovers. A tough, no nonsense defender, "Faz" tackled confidently and very rarely mis-timed a challenge.

After giving 18 years loyal service to the club as a player Fazackerley left to pursue coaching ambitions. Won great acclaim during a spell with Newcastle before joining the Ewood back room staff - most recently employed as a coach to Kevin Keegan's England squad.

Simon Garner

With 168 league goals Simon Garner was without doubt the most prolific striker in the history of the club. Over 14 years Garner became the darling of the fans after making his debut in 1976.

Garner was a quick, instinctive finisher who would snap up any half chance that fell in and around the box. Scored goals of all types and was truly prolific but, alas, never got the chance to show himself at the very top level.

Alan Shearer

The star turn when Rovers stunned the soccer world to take the Premiership title in 1995, Alan Shearer was brought to Rovers by Kenny Dalglish after promotion to the top flight in 1992 and many felt that at £3m he was 'expensive'!

Shearer was widely regarded as the complete striker, strong, quick and able to score from anywhere. After setting countless Premiership goalscoring records he moved to Newcastle in 1996 for a world record £15 million fee.

In his pomp considered the best all-round striker in Europe, Shearer will always have a special place in the Ewood Hall of Fame.

Fans' Stories

Fans' Stories

Frank Leigh Speaking

When Frank Leigh says he has seen it all at Ewood Park....his claim is on safe ground.

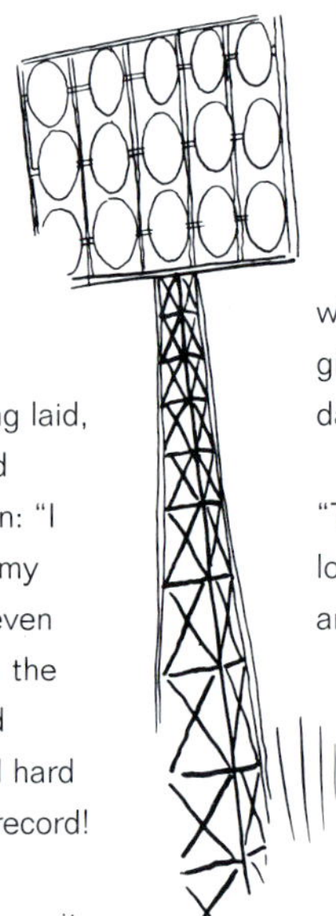

For Frank, a Rovers fan for almost eight decades, visited Ewood every single day during the major re-building project of the early '90s.

He watched every brick being laid, every pole being pitched and every nail being hammered in: "I saw it all, spending most of my waking time down there - I even got on first name terms with the builders and they even joked about awarding me a special hard hat to mark my attendance record!

"I live just around the corner, so it wasn't far to go. Whenever they finished part of the ground the builders would say "Frank, have you been in here yet?"

Often, I would be one of the first people to go in the new boardroom, or in the changing rooms. It was quite an experience.

"I remember when they lowered the roof onto the Darwen End, I was standing alongside the guy in charge, watching with him as the huge cranes moved a truly giant structure into position. It may sound daft but it was quite a moving experience.

"That's my baby, finished," he said. The look on his face was one I can't explain, and he couldn't put into words what he was feeling. That's how I feel about the club. There is nothing like it.

"One day when they ripped down the famous old Nuttall Street Stand, I went over and picked up a brick from the rubble - well I had to have a souvenir didn't I!"

Frank has been watching Rovers since the tender age of six.

Top:
The enormous stand arrives in parts

Bottom:
The roof is lowered on the Darwen End

"My father made quite sure there was no danger of me going off and supporting some other club. As the years went by I starting going with a few pals of mine. We met up before every game at the back of the Darwen End, as far back as you could go. That way we were high up, which was good for me because it was the only way I could see over everyone's heads being so short!

"There were 16 of us who went regularly. We had our fun, there was the usual banter from the terraces but it was always light-hearted, there was never any nastiness."

60 Played at both centre forward and centre half and had the nickname "Tex" - name him

(Terry Eccles)

Left:
The Nuttall Street Stand entrance

"My father was a true Roverite and he used to help out training the club's A-team so I often went down and trained with them. Sometimes I watched and sometimes I ran the line but there were also the times when they were a man short, for instance if a trialist didn't turn up. Those were the afternoons I looked forward to, because I would have to make up the numbers!

"I remember one time when we were due to play against Chorley. I wasn't expecting to play, but it turned out that they couldn't raise a team. They asked my Dad if I could fill in, and I ended up playing up front against Rovers. We won as well, 4-2!

"After the match Chorley asked me if I could sign for them, but my father didn't even let me answer. There was no way he was going to let me sign for anyone except Rovers.

"That's how I was brought up, Rovers through and through. That's why I love the club so much and I have never lost my enthusiasm. Even when I got married and long before the advent of television, my wife would know without having to ask if Rovers had lost. I would be so miserable when I walked through the door that it was pretty obvious! I'm not the kind of person who can just laugh it off and think, "Well, never mind."

"On those occasions, she would know I wouldn't be wanting any tea. Our house would be pretty quiet for the rest of the evening! I consider myself the sort of fan who will shout and cheer until his throat hurts - rarely critical of my team and never abusive towards opponents. For some folk a football match is 'us against them' on the terraces and in the stands, as well as on the pitch. Not for me though.

"The way I see it, if someone else wants to do for their team what I do for Rovers, fair enough. There was never any trouble between supporters when I started watching football, that wasn't our way.

"These days I think a lot of fans are cheering Rovers goals because they feel like they've got one over on the fans at the other end of the ground. That's not how it should be.

"Look back a few decades and football had a much more homely, friendly atmosphere. I've stood next to opposition fans on the terraces without the slightest hint of any bother. That would be unheard of these days. There are police and stewards everywhere now, but back then they weren't needed.

61 England youth international striker and home-grown product who seemed to score as many goals against Rovers as for them during an illustrious career! Who?
(John Byrom)

62 How old was Ronnie Clayton when he made his league debut for Rovers against QPR in 1951?
(16)

Left:
The stand dwarfs the workmen

Right:
Frank Leigh today

"Players were more accessible back then, but nowadays they don't seem to acknowledge the fans the same. I was lucky that through family connections I got to know the players better than most. Derek Dougan, for example, was often in our house before a game. You would never see any of the players mixing with the supporters like that now."

But although he preferred the way football was when he was younger, Frank recognises the fact that there are some advantages to the modern game.

"Players nowadays are worth a lot of money, so they are well-looked after. As a result they become better and the pace at which the game is played is amazing. I really don't think many of the stars of yesterday would have kept up with the lads of today.

"I can't stand it when people say players have it easy. They may get a lot of money, maybe too much, but they work hard for it, especially when you think of the pressure they are under. I can see why people think they earn too much, a lot of them get the same in a week as what most fans earn in a year - but who is to blame for that, certainly not the players."

Fans' Stories

Norman Barton: 1928 And All That.....

Few people can remember Rovers lifting the FA Cup....only a handful can claim to have been there to see it happen!

Norman Barton is among that number.

From his home in Ribchester, 90 year-old Norman - a fan since he was 10 - looks back on his own special Wembley experience of way back in 1928 when Rovers beat odds-on favourites Huddersfield Town.

"We beat Newcastle in the semi-final and, like everyone else, I obviously wanted to go to Wembley. But tickets were that hard to come by I gave up on the idea pretty quickly.

"Then I had a stroke of luck. I was 19 at the time and the night before the game I was at a local Conservative club. Just before closing time a friend of mine came in and said he had two tickets - I couldn't believe my luck!"

Table-topping Huddersfield were chasing their second successive league title. Rovers, hovering somewhere near the bottom, weren't given a chance.

"When I told my Dad I was going to Wembley he told me not to bother, even he was so sure we'd lose! Everyone was writing us off, but we hadn't gone all the way down there for nothing and neither had the players.

"We had to catch a train at six in the morning straight to Wembley. When we got off the train we walked along the famous Wembley Way and there were already hundreds of people there. It was a marvellous occasion, truly memorable.

"When we got inside the ground it was quite unbelievable. There were bands playing, the fans were cheering away, and then we all sang "Abide With Me." It was an incredible atmosphere, I can't describe how it felt to be part of it all. I doubt anyone can."

Norman can still remember the full line-up that day, and has no trouble recalling the goals that won the famous trophy.

"The game was without doubt one of the best I have ever seen. We shocked Huddersfield with a goal in the first minute when Thornewell centred and Roscamp knocked the lot in the net - ball and goalkeeper!

"It wasn't long before they made it 2-0. Tommy McLean wasn't really noted for his shooting ability, but he cracked one in from what must have been 20 yards! After that, Huddersfield started a bit of a fightback. They managed to pull one back but Roscamp scored again to make it safe."

"It was magnificent to see Rovers walking up the famous steps and when Harry Healless lifted the cup there was such a loud cheer it was like a bomb had gone off!

"We were on top of the world. There haven't been too many times in my life I've been happier than that."

Eventually it was time to go home, but not before they had taken time to celebrate the victory!

63 What was Rovers' best Division Two finish of the 50s?

(2nd (57/58))

64 Tommy Briggs scored more than 30 goals for Rovers in how many consecutive seasons?

(4)

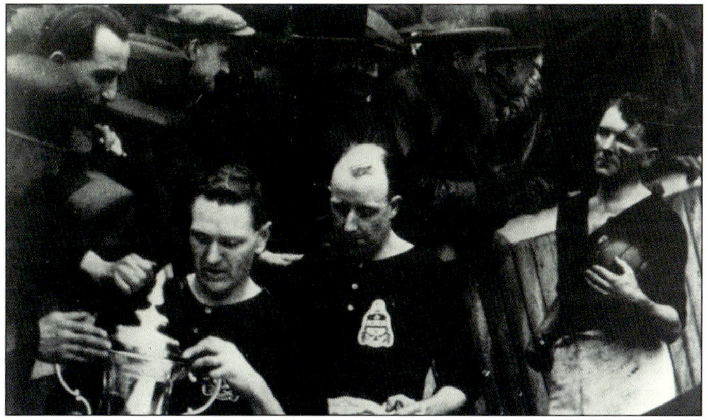

Far left
Harry Healless - Captain of Blackburn Rovers' Cup winning team in 1928

Left:
Harry Healless receiving the FA Cup in 1928

Below:
Norman Barton today

"Oh yes, we had a drink and went sightseeing around London, nothing too crazy but we enjoyed it all the same. It was midnight when we caught the train home, and although we were still in high spirits we were all exhausted and most of the Rovers fans on the train were asleep!"

Back in Blackburn the next morning, Norman was the centre of attention.

"Everyone was asking what it was like but I was lost for words. You can't put something like that into words. I was describing the goals and explaining how the day went, but you really have to experience something like that for yourself."

The memorable win set Rovers on course for three straight league victories in the following weeks.

"At that time the cup final wasn't the last game of the season and we played Portsmouth three days later. Winning the cup did us a power of good, because on the back of six league defeats in a row, we managed to win - 6-0!"

65 Who knocked Rovers out of the 1957/58 FA Cup after a semi final played at Maine Road?

(Bolton)

66 Who did Rovers send crashing out of the 1959/60 FA Cup in a quarter final replay at Ewood Park?

(Burnley)

Fans' Stories

Ray Barratt: 1930s

Right: Letter from BRFC asking Tomlinson when he expects to be 'demobbed'

Training sessions for Rovers stars of the 1930s - Bob Pryde, Arnold Whiteside, Len Butt and Co - were invariably held on Little Wembley, little more than a course, cinder pad of a pitch sited at the back of the Blackburn End where now stands a spacious car park.

Goalposts were painted on the adjoining weaving shed wall and dust, kicked up off the uneven surface, was a consistent enemy, especially for the goalkeeping fraternity.

Young boys gathered daily to watch their heroes put through their paces and Ray Barratt was among that number.

Ray was still a year or two short of his teens when the Second World War broke out but, even by then, the young Blackburn schoolboy, one of five brothers, had already forged a close affinity with his home-town football club.

His first experience of Ewood Park came in 1934 - a Thursday afternoon reserve team match. He was hooked - and still is.

The love affair has never wavered and Ray still has a daily commitment to the club, carrying out a variety of duties behind the scenes.

His father, who died when Ray was just seven, built radios out of a small shop on Audley Range. The family later moved to Malvern Avenue and Ray still lives within kicking distance of Ewood on Bolton Road.

"I have always been able to walk from home to the ground - mind you, in my early days of watching most of the players walked here too, or came by bike or jumped on a tram.

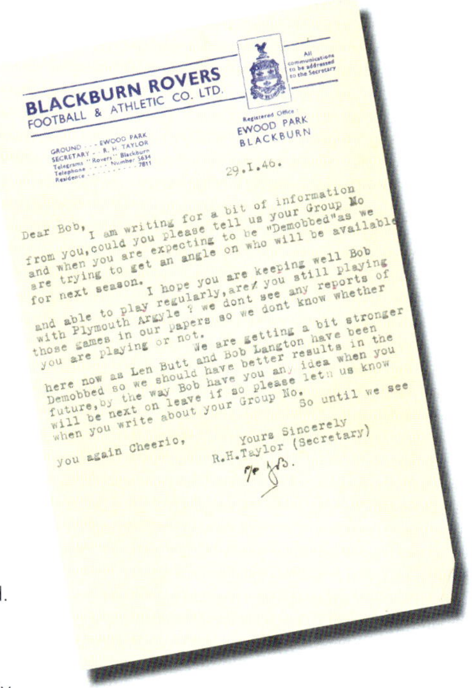
BLACKBURN ROVERS
FOOTBALL & ATHLETIC CO. LTD.

All communications to be addressed to the Secretary

GROUND - - - EWOOD PARK
SECRETARY - - R. H. TAYLOR
Telegrams "Rovers" Blackburn
Telephone - - - - Number 5634
Residence - - - - - - - 7811

Registered Office:
EWOOD PARK
BLACKBURN

29.I.46.

Dear Bob,
I am writing for a bit of information from you, could you please tell us your Group No and when you are expecting to be "Demobbed" as we are trying to get an angle on who will be available for next season.

I hope you are keeping well Bob and able to play regularly, are you still playing with Plymouth Argyle ? we dont see any reports of those games in our papers so we dont know whether you are playing or not.

We are getting a bit stronger here now as Len Butt and Bob Langton have been Demobbed so we should have better results in the future, by the way Bob have you any idea when you will be next on leave if so please let us know when you write about your Group No.

So until we see you again Cheerio,

Yours Sincerely
R.H.Taylor (Secretary)

"It was totally different and hard to explain, particularly to youngsters who have only ever known today's football and today's footballers.

"There seemed more togetherness then, more loyalty and more fun. I knew England internationals who earned £2-a-week plus a couple of quid for a win and a quid for a draw. They combined playing here with part-time jobs - some even got up at 5.30am and did things like paper rounds. Can you imagine that?

"But they were real people and always had time for the lads down at training. Not that they could get away - there were no fast cars, no escaping our attentions. But we never felt we were getting on their nerves.

"They would turn up about 10am and trained for two to two-and-a-half hours. When it finished they chatted with us, got changed and went up into town.

"I remember that during my days at St Alban's Higher Grade there used to be complimentary tickets issued by Rovers. The teachers would hand them out on the Friday before home games to the kids who had done well, tried hard or not missed a day off school

67 How many Rovers players started all 42 league matches and all six FA Cup games in the 1957/58 season?
(3)

68 Rovers recorded their all-time record league victory in November 1954. The score was 9-0 but who did they beat?
(Middlesbrough)

Left:
Souvenir matchbox of BRFC. Winners of the English Cup, played at Wembley, April 21st 1928. Blackburn Rovers 3 Huddersfield Town 1

Below:
Ray Barratt today

"Admission was about threepence but when you couldn't afford it or you didn't have a comp, you waited until the queues were at their longest before sneaking between the legs and under the turnstiles!

"I always got involved in bits of jobs around the place. A friend of the family had a small outlet behind some cottages on Livesey Branch Road which he used to open up on match-days for people to park their bikes. I helped run that for a while and we regularly stored up to 30 cycles which the chap used to say paid for a bit of tripe for his tea!

"I remember the team had a mascot too, who used to walk around the outside of the pitch with a blue and white budgie in a cage. You couldn't get many souvenirs in those days, nothing was on sale here, apart from a fellow with a board crammed full with rosettes - for both teams.

"But one of the club's directors, Johnny Forbes, who had a sports shop in town, stocked a few bits and bats, scarves and such like but nothing compared to what is around now.

Under the management of one Bob Crompton, Rovers were a mid-table First Division outfit at the dawn of the thirties playing in front of average home crowds of around 15,000.

In 1936 they suffered the disappointment of relegation, finishing rock bottom after losing 8-1 twice, at West Brom and Wolves.

But they returned three years later as Second Division champions and Ray can still trot out the line-up to this day.

"It was a damn good side, Bob Pryde, Walter Crook, Jack Weddle, Len Butt and Nobby Clarke.

"It was a great shame that they never got the chance to make an impact in the top flight for after three games of the 1939-40 season war broke out and the Football League closed down. But no-one can take your memories away and I still smile when I look back. My proudest moment as a Rovers fan was in seeing the club win the Premier League in 1995, but those early days were very memorable too. Happy times."

Fans' Stories

Bryan Barlow: 1950s

For many this was Rovers golden era - not, perhaps, in terms of trophies in the Ewood cabinet but certainly in terms of flair, excitement, entertainment and some true legends.

People will always talk in terms of Ronnie Clayton and Bryan Douglas - and quite right too for the duo shone bright for both club and country, clocking up more than 1000 Rovers appearances and winning some 71 England caps between them.

But for Bryan Barlow, an Ewood die-hard who cut his teeth on fifties football, there was another Rovers star who personified the era.........one Thomas Henry Briggs.

A generic, burly centre-forward for whom goals were never a problem, Tommy epitomised the club's famous fighting spirit and was a crowd pleaser from day one, bagging two goals on his first game at Ewood Park.

He went on to score 30 goals in four successive seasons and on a memorable February afternoon in 1955 he created a club record by scoring seven in a single game!

Little wonder such heroics left an impression on fans likes Bryan, then a teenager.

As a young Darwener Bryan would hop on the merry-go-round of Blackburn Transport double-deckers that ran a continuous circle from the town centre to Cravens Brow.

His father carried the flask (usually containing more rum than coffee!) but Bryan was invariably parted from parental supervision by the sway of the crowd.

"Once you had queued up and squeezed in you just seemed to get carried along on a sea of people. Where you ended up was often down to luck rather than choice but it was just a pleasure and privilege to be there and see it all unfolding before your eyes," Bryan recalls.

Aside from Clayton's silky skills and Duggie ruling the right flank, the fans of the fifties also had a great affinity with the likes of Briggs.

"Come Saturday afternoon all we wanted was to see the goals flying in and you could bet your last penny that if Briggs got within striking distance the only touch the keeper would get would be in pulling it out of the net.

"He was never the most skilful footballer but the order of the day was a bulldozer of a centre-forward who could bundle the ball home - a description written for Tommy."

So where was Bryan's hero when Rovers recorded one of their most spectacular and memorable victories against Middlesbrough in 1954?

"I couldn't believe it. After a slow start we just started smashing goals in one after the other. First Eddie Quigley belted home a rebound, then Eddie Crossan did the same. Quigley scored again, then Frank Mooney, then Quigley hit his hat-trick. Five-nil up at half-time was a shock but not to see Briggs' name on the scoresheet was even more surprising."

69 Tommy Johnston scored how many of the eight goals that Rovers put past Newcastle United in the 1958/59 season?

(five)

70 How many league games did it take Rovers to record their first victory of the 1951/52 season?

(ten)

Rovers went on to put another four past Middlesbrough via Crossan, Mooney and Bobby Langton to write their way into the Ewood record books - a feat that remains unsurpassed today.

But not to be outdone, later that very same season Bryan witnessed Tommy going all-out to better that momentous win.....all on his own - well nearly!

Early February and not the most pleasant of winter afternoons, 25,000 pairs of eyes watched Briggs fire a staggering SEVEN goals past a hapless Bristol Rovers to book his own special place in Rovers' folklore.

"He certainly made up for the Boro game with that display. His performance that day summed up all that Tommy stood for - receiving brilliant service from all over the field and banging in the goals from every angle with the greatest of ease.

"After the game even the other players applauded him off the field, which emphasised what an awesome impression he had made."

As the fifties wore on, Bryan, approaching the twilight of his teens, decided to position himself on the Spion Kop (a corner of the ground between the Darwen End and the Riverside Stand). It was from that bustling vantage point that he watched Rovers bundle arch rivals Burnley out of the 1959/60 FA Cup en route to the Final.

After drawing 3-3 at Turf Moor, the Clarets descended on Ewood for a replay which pulled in a staggering 54,000 attendance.

"There was probably more to shout about in that game than in the actual Final itself. Peter Dobing and Ally MacLeod scored the goals which got us to Wembley but knocking Burnley out made the win even more satisfying. We might have lost the Final but at least we put one over on the Clarets!"

The Spion Kop wasn't the only placc that Bryan got to see his Ewood heroes, though...thanks to people like Eric Bell, another hero of the decade and another Darwener to boot!

Bell stayed loyal to the cause for 11 years despite being forced to compete with golden boy Clayton for a place in the half-back line.

"The players were much more accessible back then...stars like Bill Eckersley travelled to games on the same bus as the fans.

"Eric Bell had a post office just a few doors up from our house in Redearth Road and he was just as happy to talk football as sell stamps.

"Autograph-hunting was so much easier because almost all the players lived in or around Blackburn and it was no surprise to stroll past them in the street. They were still big celebrities in the eyes of the fans but it didn't seem to put them out of our reach.

"They could even be found freely mixing and socialising with supporters in local pubs on Saturday nights, chatting about the game. It was a wonderful introduction to football watching and I will always look back on the 1950s with great pleasure."

Above:
Bryan Barlow today

71 In which North West town was 1950's star Eddie Quigley born?
(Bury)

72 En route to the 1960 FA Cup final, who did Rovers eject in the semi-final?
(Sheffield Wednesday)

Fans' Stories
Dan Talbot: 1960s

The swinging 60s was a time for change.

People changed, politics changed, and, if you believe life-long Rovers fan Dan Talbot, football changed too - dramatically.

"Although the 60s was my favourite footballing era, it was also quite a sad one," Dan remembers.

"The maximum wage was abolished, which a lot of players were happy about, but it was damaging for the game at large.

"Previously, a footballers incentive was to remain loyal to a club and hope to be well looked after. Since the abolition of the maximum wage, however, prerogatives changed. Now most players simply look around for the best deal, which has, in turn, brought about the demise of many a good club.

"In the early 60's, everyone earned the same wage, but suddenly players could earn five times what certain teams were prepared to pay them. Rovers were one of the clubs who fell behind, and were eventually relegated.

"It wasn't just us, though. Brighton were in Cup Finals back then, look at them now. It is very sad that money can affect football so much.

Despite the growth of the financial side of football, Dan still remembers the 60s fondly.

"It was the decade that I was happiest as a fan because we got into the FA Cup Final. Unfortunately Dave Whelan broke his leg, and Mick McGrath gave away an own goal! Obviously it was disappointing to lose, but it was still very special.

Right:
A selection of 1960s' tickets

"The players rode into town on an open top bus and received the same welcome they would have done if they had brought the cup home with them.

"It was a fantastic achievement, the people of Blackburn were just so happy that their team had been involved in the FA Cup Final."

The early 60s was a great time to be a Rovers fan. Dan recalls a team packed with internationals and challenging for honours.

"We had many terrific players. The likes of Bryan Douglas, Matt Woods, Harry Leyland, Fred Else, Bill Eckersley, Keith Newton all fantastic footballers.

"But my favourite player from that time was definitely Ronnie Clayton. When Rovers were relegated at the end of the 1965-66 season he had 35 England caps, but he still stayed at Ewood.

73 Which Rovers legend was the only man to play all 42 league games in the 1964/65 campaign?
(Bryan Douglas)

74 How many goals did Rovers score in the 1969/70 FA Cup competition?
(none)

"He should be held up as an example to players nowadays. He captained England but he never wanted to leave Rovers even after we went down. That sort of thing is unheard of these days."

Dan greatly appreciates the loyalty that players like Clayton showed to the club.

"Moving towards the end of the 60s you can look at Derek Fazackerley, who turned out to be a great servant to the club. If you look at the players who were here at that time, lots of them stayed longer than 10 years, whereas now that would be seen as something to be celebrated. It wasn't just players either, managers stayed put longer.

According to Dan, the thing he misses most about football back then is the match-day atmosphere. There were no hooligans, and being a fan was a much more relaxed, simple task.

"Facilities were nowhere near as good but the club had a real family feel to it. There were no fast-food outlets next door to Ewood Park, you had to settle for a hot pie and a brew, but that was great, there was something homely about it. The club shop was a front room in a house, it doesn't get much more homely than that!

"The attitude the fans had towards each other was different as well. Obviously there was friendly rivalry, but never any thuggery.

"It was unheard of for fans to rip up seats or throw bottles. You would come out of the ground talking to the opposition fans, never even thinking that any trouble might start because football just wasn't like that then. I've stood next to opposing fans on terraces, with no bother.

"You could take the kids down and have a nice family day out. You didn't see many police around because they weren't needed. You didn't need stewards or anything like that.

"You just stood on the terraces and shouted for the team, hoped you won, then went home."

Right:
Dan Talbot today

75 Who had the longest managerial reign at Ewood in the 60s?
(Jack Marshall)

Fans' Stories

David Barker: 1970s

Top Right: Blackburn Rovers' Travel Club 1974/75 goes to Swindon

Right: Illustration by David Barker, age 9

Satin scarves, footballers with bubble perms and draughts which took your breath away when standing on the terraces in flares.

Football in the 1970s during which Rovers suffered not one but two relegation seasons involving the (old) Third Division - low points in a rollercoaster record.

But through it all the fans kept the faith, fans like David Barker, of Wheelton, one of the diehards who stayed the course, both home and away.

His first game, aged just nine, was at Rovers' 4-0 win over Millwall in September 1969, but it wasn't long before he was taking to the road. He even made it to Cambridge on that fateful day in 1974 - making him one of a very select band.

"Rovers always commanded a strong support, especially away from home. In fact the away travel club is to my knowledge the first in the country. It made away travel more accessible to a lot of people so there was always a strong crowd urging them on.

"We had our own train, the Ewood Express, which went all over the country, and of course the League Liner was up and running in those days. It was a big thing to get the League Liner at the club because it was mainly used for top division teams...it was because of Rovers' phenomenal support that we got it so many times.

"We had the Liner for an away trip to Cambridge, which is a hell of a trip at the best of times, so of course we were delighted. But the week before Gordon Lee had sold Tony Field - the Alan Shearer of Division Three - and it knocked the wind out of the club.

"There were only 150 of us who made use of the Liner in the end. We won 2-0, I remember the game especially because it was snowing in Blackburn when we left, and when we got to Cambridge it was so hot we all had ice cream!"

But there were other trials and tribulations, not all of them connected with football.

There was the Trade Union movement to consider!

76 Which Ewood hero made his debut against Chelsea on September 19th 1960 and went on to make more than 350 appearances for the club?

(Keith Newton)

77 Apart from the luckless Rovers defender Mick McGrath who scored for Wolves in the 1960 FA Cup Final?

(Norman Deeley, 2)

"The power strikes affected a lot of matches - there was a timetable which told you which areas would be blacked out and when, and if Blackburn were at home on that night you knew you'd lost your floodlights!

"They started switching a lot of those games to weekday afternoons instead, and I remember seeing Willington play in an FA Cup replay and we hammered them 6-1. Ken Furphy came down the tunnel at the end of the game and came straight over to me and my mate: "Why aren't you two at school!" he roared.

"It actually sounds really quaint when you think of it now, but the fans could get much closer to the team in those days."

Literally in many cases. For starters, fencing didn't start coming in until the mid- seventies, which meant the average fan could - and often did - run onto the field of play.

"Before the fences went up you'd find yourself on the pitch, if not at the end then during the game, especially if the TV cameras were there. Thousands of fans would run onto the pitch, not just to celebrate a goal, but to get on the telly. Players physically threw fans off the pitch!

"But when football started to get a reputation for hooliganism fences went up all over the country and it was no different at Ewood.

"Because the old enclosure was more expensive to stand in we devised a technique to nick under the fences when there were no police watching! We would try and get into all four sides during the course of a game, and up into the stands as well.

Left:
David's Travel Club card

Below:
David's Scrapbook

"Away from home a lot of fans used to hang about around the main entrance of whatever ground, wearing their Rovers scarves, waiting for directors or players to give them their spare complimentary tickets. Amazingly it worked almost every time!"

But aside from all the hooliganism, the fencing and the changing face of football, there were some fine displays on the field. And even though those golden moments were perhaps more spartan than they had been 20 years previously, there were nevertheless enough of them to keep David loyal for the last 30 years.

"I suppose I started watching Rovers at the start of the downward spiral, so when we won promotion in 1975 the atmosphere was incredible. After so many years of terrible football, to get promotion was a great boost.

"That's not to say we didn't have good players though. David Wagstaffe was my all time hero, and I can still picture him scoring against Burnley at Ewood Park in the Anglo-Scottish Cup.

"The rapport he had with the fans, even in the twilight of his career was just incredible. People go on about Alan Shearer, but Waggy was idolised. He was a winger so he used to have to run right across the pitch to the old Riverside stand. He'd shake hands with people, give kids footballs - and he was a decent player too.

Blackburn Rovers F.C. Ltd.

Scroll of Honour

"RUN FOR THE ROVERS"

We certify that the person below completed 11. sponsored laps of Ewood Park thus helping to raise the amount of £450.00 for and on behalf of Blackburn Rovers Football Club, during season 1973/1974

Name DAVID BARKER.

Address 35, KENYON LANE, WHEELTON

Age 14 yrs.

Dated this 18th day of APRIL. 1974

Signed

"When he was transferred to Blackpool me and my mates were gutted. It felt like losing every single girlfriend you'd ever had on one night. We wrote a letter to him saying you can't leave, and he even wrote back to us - not that it made any difference.

"He was part of the Jim Smith team, which was superb: Kevin Hird and John Bailey at full back, David Wagstaffe and Noel Brotherston on the wing...a superb attacking force which just lacked the forwards to finish the job off!

"Tony Field was another player worth a mention. I'd been watching Rovers for about four years when he arrived - he was quick, strong and could take the ball around virtually everyone. I missed out on Bryan Douglas, but Field was very special too - he excited you and scored some great goals."

"The old club shop was built into the Nuttall Street Stand, and it was like going into the chippy! I used to go in every couple weeks for the away programme from the previous match, and there was just one long counter in it. A very limited range of things in it - one or two metal badges and a couple of scarves. We used to get the Rovers satin scarves which were huge back then, but you had to be very careful with them because the writing always scratched off, especially if it got crumpled up!

"Chorley Supporters Club, of which I was a member, used to have fundraising events like sponsored walks - Gordon Lee once presented us with a certificate after we had done a sponsored run around the perimeter for Ewood Park! We had a few walks though, setting off from Chorley in the morning to be at Ewood Park in time for the game. It's daft to think of fans raising money for the club now, but there was no Jack Walker back then, and the effort really was appreciated. Dave Whelan once set us off after he opened his first shop in Chorley."

Above:
David Barker's Sponsored Run Certificate

Far Left:
David Barker today

Fans' Stories

George Hatton: 1980s

The 1980s was a frustrating time to be a Rovers fan. This was the decade when the 'nearly men' tag arrived - and stuck!

Rovers narrowly missed out on promotion four times. George Hatton, of Livesey, squirmed through it all.....

"Being a Rovers fan even in the 1980s was vastly different to nowadays," says George.

"Apart from the playing side of things we had no facilities or leisure amenities. For example, the club shop was just a room in a house on Nuttall Street, very modest by today's standards. I think the total stock came to about £2,500, whereas nowadays it would probably come to about £2.5 million!"

George was a season ticket holder in the old Nuttall Street Stand. He remembers those Saturday afternoons with a nostalgic smile on his face.

"There were seats at the back that came down to the directors' box. Either side of the tunnel were the Darwen and Blackburn End enclosures, which were terraced.

"When Bob Saxton was the manager he used to sit in the directors' box, between the fans and the players. I have many memories of him hurling abuse back at the fans who were berating his players!

"It was an old fashioned stand, it wouldn't have looked out of place in the 1940's. Even the seats were rickety, and there was very little leg room. Nobody had even thought about Health and Safety. Nowadays you have to be able to evacuate the ground in five minutes flat. I think it would have taken about a week and a half to empty that stand!

"The food was a football cliche in itself. There was a certain amount of choice, you could have potato pie or potato pie. There was a choice of coffee, Bovril or coffee and Bovril - and we counted ourselves lucky for that!"

George fondly remembers the days when being a Rovers fan meant being part of the club itself.

"The best thing about being a Rovers fan in the 80's was the relationship between the club and the supporters. At the beginning of the 1990's the two drifted apart, but at that time Rovers was still a family club. The players and managers had time for the fans.

"Some people would think that strange, that the fans were closer to the club when it was not doing as well. But the excitement at being almost there is a lot more passionate than when you are there. When it's been done, you just sit back and relax."

78 Who scored Rovers first and last league goals of the 1961/62 season?

(They were both penalties) (Bryan Douglas)

79 Before being promoted to the Premier League in 1992, when was the last time Rovers played top-flight football?

(1965-66)

"Players and managers were more approachable, that's what I miss. They weren't prima-donnas like they are now, they were charismatic and actually very nice people, players like Derek Fazackerley, Glenn Keeley, Tony Parkes and Duncan McKenzie.

"Younger fans might not believe this, but Simon Garner was held in greater esteem in Blackburn than Alan Shearer was in his time here, because he had the charisma. Simon Garner was a Blackburn Rovers player seven days a week, but Shearer was only a Rovers player for 90 minutes a week. Noel Brotherston lived on Buncer Lane, ten minutes from the ground, these days players don't even want to live in Blackburn. These were players who were part of the community, and most importantly, they played for Rovers, not themselves.

"A good word to describe the club in the 80s would be homely. People talk about that sort of atmosphere being lost around the 70s, but I still knew it then. People were more forgiving and charitable towards the players, mainly because you felt like you knew them personally.

"Throughout the decade Rovers were the nearly men. In the early 80s we missed out on promotion on goal difference, then there were another three play-off failures. Obviously it was a frustrating time, but the fans never turned on the players.

Despite all the disappointments and near misses, George remembers one time when Rovers fans were on top of the world.

"I suppose the highlight of the 80s was the Full Members Cup win in 1987. It was called a Mickey Mouse competition, but that isn't how the people of Blackburn saw it. There were 40,000 people at Wembley that day, 30,000 from Blackburn and only 10,000 from Charlton, which was about five minutes down the road!

"The town shut down for the day. The club brought coaches in from all over the North of England, Newcastle, Yorkshire, even from Scotland, and they were all filled. This was at a time when Rovers only pulled in crowds of 8,000 for home games, it was phenomenal. That win might not have meant more to Rovers fans than the Championship win in '95, but it was celebrated better, and people enjoyed it more because it was such a sweet victory. Who were we to win a Wembley cup final? Also, the players celebrated with the fans. They had won it for Blackburn and they were proud of it. In '95 the players were nowhere to be seen."

One of the most important things to George as a Rovers fan is his second home, Ewood Park.

"To see how quickly Rovers have progressed you only have to look at the ground. The Walkersteel stand was the best one then, it put the others to shame. Now, they can't tear it down quickly enough because it's outdated.

"There's no denying that the place was, for want of a better word, a dump. Fans were paying top dollar for an inferior service, as they were all over the country, not just here. Sunderland had the same problem, Roker Park was badly in need of some work. To their credit, Rovers have never been the kind of club to let that go. As soon as the money became available a little later, the fans were given the stadium they deserved."

Despite having little money, Rovers always maintained their status in Division Two. To do that, there had to be some very shrewd management.

"Up to around 1987 Saxton was in charge. This was a time when Rovers had to survive on a shoestring budget. He was brought in because he was an experienced lower division manager who had a proven track record working with very little money. He did the deals that made people scratch their heads and wonder how he did it. Terry Gennoe, for example, came to Rovers for £60,000 and he was as good even when he retired as most Premiership goalkeepers are now.

"Saxton also re-vamped the youth policy at the club. Rovers were in grave danger of following in Burnley's footsteps, because they would bring young talent through and then sell it straight away. Seeing Burnley almost fall out of the league that way, Saxton nipped it in the bud before the same thing happened to us. We started keeping hold of the players, people like Simon Barker, who is still playing.

"However, the down side to signing players for next to nothing was that it made Rovers look unambitious. Don MacKay was fortunate in that the first thing he did when he came here was win the Full Members Cup. That immediately raised the profile of the club, and paved the way for Rovers to sign people like Steve Archibald and Ossie Ardiles.

"When that happened, Jack Walker was sat in the background, and when people started to take notice of Rovers I think he got more and more ambitious for the club. Suddenly Match Of The Day cameras started appearing at the games and while this was all great for the fans, it ended up being MacKay's down fall - basically the club outgrew him."

Left:
Ipswich v Rovers, Simon Garner's shot comes to nothing

Below:
George Hatton today

80 How many goals did Fred Pickering score for Rovers during his two spells with the club, 54, 74, 94?
(74)

81 Who was Rovers top scorer in the 1969/70 season?
(Don Martin)

Fans' Stories

Jon West: 1990s

"be careful when choosing your football club son.... it will be with you for the rest of your life"

Above: Ouch! Simon Garner shoots for goal

Facing Page Left: Mike Newell celebrates

Facing Page Right: Jon West today

Jon West was only part way through primary school when he "discovered" Rovers.

But what he witnessed, a triumphant return to the top flight of English football, got him firmly on the hook - probably forever.

Jon, 16, of Great Harwood, is one of the soccer class of the 90s - those for whom Sky television has always been the norm - who have ridden the Rovers rollercoaster with relish.

A fully paid up member of the blue and white army since the beginning of the decade - Jon watched in awe as Rovers made headline news not once but twice in his first few years, winning promotion via the play-off's in 1992 and coming top of the Premiership pile in 1995.

He went a few times before that - dad, Peter, is a supporter too: "I have memories of the Second Division days before Kenny Dalglish, but not particularly clear ones. Simon Garner was the big hero and I remember he scored most of the time, but I can't recall any of the goals."

All that changed when Dalglish rode into town.

For most supporters, King Kenny's arrival sparked the greatest chapter in Rovers' post war history.

"Players came in who I had actually heard of, " he says. "People like Alan Wright, Tim Sherwood, Mike Newell and Roy Wegerle.

"But David Speedie is the one man who we all looked up to - the club even started a lottery game called the Speedie Return to celebrate his return from suspension...now that is true fame!

There are a variety of reasons why John could have picked up with Rovers at the tail end of the 1980s - tradition locality, chance, boredom, peer pressure and bullying. But he could have ventured elsewhere.....

"Most of my dad's football watching was done on The Kop at Liverpool.
It was ironic that it was actually in a match against Liverpool that he - and I - switched allegiances.

"It was an FA Cup tie and while I started the game a fan of the reds I ended a true blue and white. Back then, Rovers were never on Match of the Day or in sticker albums and you certainly couldn't get any Rovers' players in plastic figures, but there was just something appealing about the club.

82 He looked like a character from Dickens - but once "banged one in" against Manchester City in a cup tie. Who?

(Jim Fryatt)

83 Born in Stockton he was Ewood manager between 1971 an 1973. Name him.

(Ken Furphy)

84 Scottish striker who spent between 1964 and 1970 at Ewood and later became player-manager at Great Harwood Town. Surname starts with a D.

(Malcolm Darling)

"My first real memories are of the promotion winning season. The Christmas after Kenny's arrival the club began a run of defeats and the promotion which had looked a formality quickly began to seem less and less likely. Thankfully the team managed to clamber back into a promotion spot - thanks to amongst other things a Speedie hat-trick on the closing day of the season - which meant that we played Derby in a two-leg play-off semi-final.

"The home leg of this fixture came first and the ground was alive with the anticipation. For the first time we had these enormous flags passed all around the Walker Steel stand which to me was all a new experience, but to many of the people there that day it was a situation they had seen before - Rovers had reached the play-offs the three seasons prior to my following of the club.

"Derby scored twice very early on in the game reducing us all to a bunch of nervous wrecks. I'm not sure how Scott Sellars scored or if anyone then cared. The fact was that he did at which point the ground erupted and that goal created the biggest rumble I had ever heard at Ewood - until that is, Mike Newell popped up with an equaliser and Speedie chipped in with two more."

"There are certain matches and moments you just never forget, Newcastle in the last home fixture of our league winning season for example..

"The tension that night was enough to give you lockjaw. The previous game had seen David Batty return to the fray along with Kevin Gallacher - both from long term injury. Sadly while Batty had managed to pull through to help the rapidly tiring side, Gallacher sustained another broken leg soon after scoring in his brief return.

"Results in general had started to fall away and this led some to question Rovers' ability to stay the pace. But Alan Shearer's header put Rovers' one-nil up in the first half and then the rest of the game was a collection of shots and saves from Peter Beardsley and Tim Flowers respectively.

"But what followed was one of the most wonderful sights I have ever witnessed at a football game. As the Walker Steel Stand left the ground they reached over the fence to the Darwen End to swop shirts with the away supporters. Rovers had displayed the "bottle" that many had thought they lacked and went on to take the crown."

"My short tenure as a loyal supporter has been nothing if not exciting, promotion, championship, relegation. But I have also witnessed many changes and, with the advent of digital TV, more changes are doubtless on the way.

"But whatever happens on the peripheries, the game always stays the same. It will always be about winning and losing, highs and lows and following your team through good times and bad.

"The game which ended our stay in the Premier League was on the same day that I stood down from school in preparation for my GCSE exams. I never thought we would go down even though we needed to beat Man. Utd. (who were heading for the Champion's League title, FA Cup and League) and then Newcastle (also in the FA final) in the final two games.

"Against the might of United we gave our all, but it wasn't enough and a goalless draw meant the result at Newcastle counted for little. We were down and it was very sad - especially for Jack Walker and the rest of the fans.

"But supporters, like players, bounce back and I believe the dawn of a new millennium will see a new awakening for Rovers."

Moving Stories

Moving Stories
Ticket To Ride

Football specials. The very phrase conjures up images of rattles, Oxo, pipes and grainy black and white pictures of leather bound balls and huge shorts.

Part of the sprawling history of football, now resigned to life in the memorabilia file, the football specials were a massive undertaking.

In the days before the M65, the turbo V8 engine and Marge Simpson air fresheners, the public transport network was a distinctly well-oiled machine. It had to be.

The streets, free of congestion, instead saw trams snaking their way round the towns buses in the 1930s - and the busiest periods were matchdays - and matchday football specials.

Blackburnian Dennis Moran, 73, worked on both the trams and the buses, including the football runs.

In the 1930s there was a waiting list of 300 men to work with Blackburn Transport, and Dennis, now based in Chesterfield, got in on the act just in time, starting work for Blackburn Borough Transport in January 1940 at the age of 15.

"The electric trams started at the turn of the century," says Dennis.

Left:
Blackburn Rovers official programme for the season 1949/50.
Oxo were not only big advertisers but an essential beverage

Below:
Dennis Moran today

"Before that the public transport system didn't service the football crowds.
There were steam and horse drawn trams around in the 19th Century, but they didn't go very far, and they didn't go down Ewood way anyway.

85 In which season did Rovers first win the Central League ?

(1964-65)

Public transport was essential for hardcore fanatics, Rovers fans braving all manner of conditions to follow Rovers around the country. On such an away trip, on January 19th 1952, 170 Rovers fans were injured - 50 of them hospitalised - and one died when the footbridge at Knowsley St Station tragically collapsed after Rovers' 2-0 win at Bury. The mayor of Blackburn and many Rovers players - including Bill Eckersley - visited many of the injured in hospital.

"Up until 1929, only trams were in operation. The trams ran solely up until 1929. Blackburn had plenty of them - and plenty of people to man them. On a matchday the morning shift started at 5am and went on until noon, when they had an hour off. The late shift started at noon instead of 2pm to cater for the crowds...the only consolation was that the crews got free admission to the game, although they had to leave well before the end to man the trams for the return journey!

"I worked a few football specials on the trams and it was easily the biggest operation of the week. The vast majority of supporters used them, although a lot still used to walk - on principal because the football specials cost a half'penny more than usual, and a lot of men objected to paying the extra!"

"The buses were introduced in the 1920's...they had 12 in 1929 and by 1935 they had 36 - a few spare for the football!

"They started running buses as football specials in 1939, starting at various pick up points in the town. The war put a stop to all that of course, and it was never re-introduced after that...from then on they only ever ran from the town centre.

"They were popular enough, but of course fuel was rationed and as far as Blackburn Transport would have been concerned a lot of it would have seemed non-essential.

"The petrol rationing after the war lasted well into the 1950s, so the football specials were understandably very popular. Besides, there were waiting lists of two years for new cars.

"The last tram ran on September 3rd 1949, when the bus fleet stood at about 120, with 20 or so at a time running on a loop from the town centre to Ewood Park and back.

"I remember one incident, a year earlier - on New Years Day 1948 - Rovers were at home to Chelsea - and we had a brand new bus. We had already picked up a load of Rovers fans when we broke down on Darwen Street bridge, right on the tram track. All the trams, carrying hundreds of fans, were all left stranded!"

Right:
Typical match transport

95

"Football specials proved a staple part of Saturday for decades, until their inevitable scaling down in the 1980s when more and more supporters were using cars to get to the match.

Left:
Tram in Trouble!

86 Who had his second spell as Rovers boss in 1970-71?

(Johnny Carey)

87 Who was the legendary Ewood goalkeeper of the 1970s recruited from Bournemouth?

(Roger Jones)

1928

1932

1946

1947

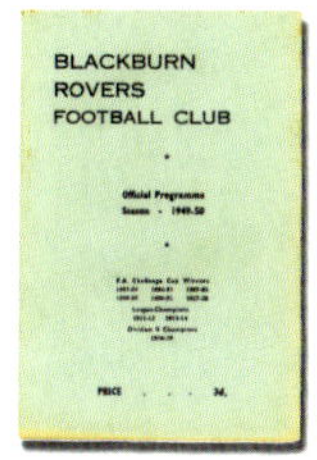

1949

1953

1957

Moving Stories

Cover Stories

Stamps, autographs, matchboxes, phone cards, shoes, toys, butterflies, debts...people collect all sorts of things for all sorts of reasons.

John Holden collects football programmes - Rovers programmes.

As stand alone historical documents, a snapshot in time, you can't beat them. Not only do they list the players, managers and opponents of the day, but the adverts - of which there were many - tell you more about the townsfolk of yesteryear than Pathé News ever could.

Like most collections, John's started off by accident: "I got into it about 13 years ago and it's grown into the thousands," says John, of Accrington.

"I used to buy the odd programme at the games and one year - I think it was 1981 - I only needed two for the full set. I hunted them down and from then on I was hooked. You do get a buzz when you complete a collection...why else would you do it?"

For an insight into the townsfolk of yesteryear? Maybe not.

For the beginner, programmes from the 1960s onwards are widespread and as a rule they're not particularly difficult to find, while programmes from the 70s and 80s can be picked up very cheaply.

But programmes more than 40 years old can be almost impossible to find, not to mention expensive.

Left:
Blackburn Rovers' smallest match programme measuring just 103mm wide and 65mm deep. Dated around 1959/60

88 Name the ex-Southport striker who became an Ewood legend in the early 70s

(Tony Field)

89 True or false - Tony Parkes once finished a season as Rovers' leading scorer?

(True)

1961

1969

1970

1974

1976

1978

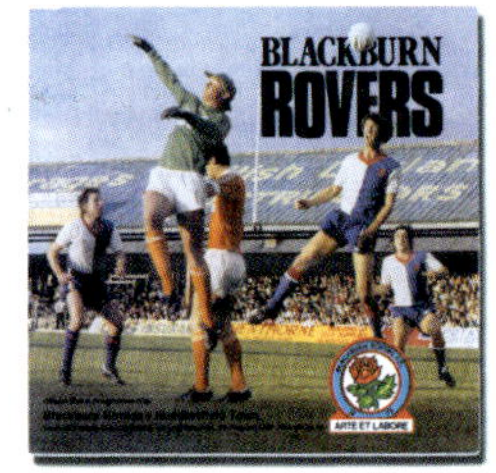

1980

Right:
During the Second World War, due to paper shortage and rationing, programmes were made from just a single sheet of thin paper, such as these pictured right, dated 1945

"There just aren't as many around. Football programmes used to be about the team, who was playing in which position. Unlike today there were no articles or features, so once you knew who was playing you would just bin it.

"Similarly, pre-war programmes are like gold dust. I know of one chap who has a programme dating back to 1914 of Blackburn v Burnley, of which there are only two known copies in the country! How do you value that!?

"The oldest Rovers programme I know about - and which still exists - dates back to a game against Sheffield Wednesday on 4th December 1909. It was 'number 14 in a new series', but only eight games into the season, and we know that programmes date back to the last century...we just don't know if they still exist or not!"

"During wartime the Rovers programmes were very basic, an A4 sheet folded in two with the teams listed. The 50s version contained more of an insight into the club, information about goings on behind the scenes, although it was still made up of adverts in the main.

"Rovers programme slowly became more and more informative with more managers notes, reviews and insights but it was the 70s when the whole thing really took off, and in 1981 the Rovers programme won the award for the best in the league."

Cunning tricks were employed however...the half-time scoreboard was a very popular ploy in the 1970s, and not just at Ewood Park. Placards were displayed around the ground at half time with half time scores from around the country cryptically encoded.

1988

1989

1989

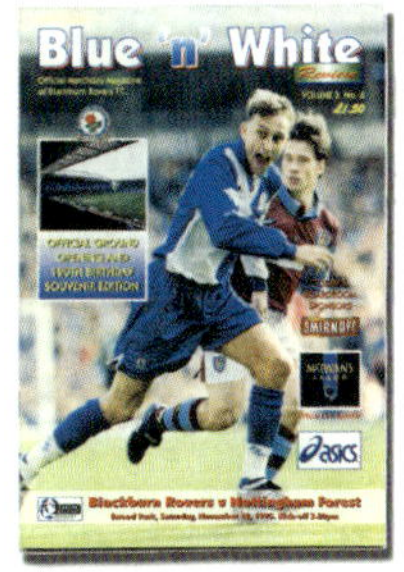

1995

1995

1998

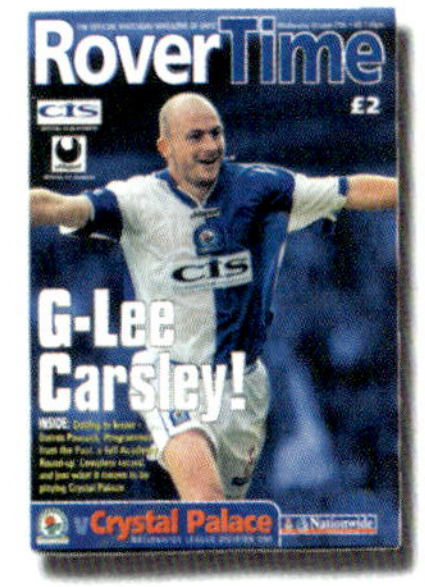

1999

To find out what "MATCH A - 3-2" meant, ensured you had to have a programme, or at least a good view of somebody elses. Sneaky.

Another popular 70s abomination more or less passed Ewood Park by. But Rovers were approached to produce a newspaper style programme, a style which had become quite fashionable among some of the trendier clubs.

But Blackburn - being north of the M25 and not quite as fashionable - kept well away, to the relief of collectors like John: "The club refused, thankfully...they would turn yellow after a week!"

That said, Rovers did produce three: against Charlton in 1975, Sheffield United and Luton (both 1978).

True to form, John's copies are all bright yellow.

Above:
1975 Centenary Souvenir Programme

Left:
John Holden

90 In 1987 Derek Fazackerley left Rovers to become player-assistant manager at which club?

(Chester City)

91 Against which club did Derek Fazackerley make his senior Rovers debut in November 1971?

(Hull City)

The Business Story

The Business Story

Two Up, Two Down

Ken Beamish was Rovers' Commercial Manager in 1986 - and worked from home!

Well.....not exactly - the four-strong Commercial Department operated out of a small terraced house on Nuttall Street.

Such were the 'demands' of the club's off-the-field activity that it warranted not a plush Blackburn End office but a basic two-up-two-down across the road.

"All we had to deal with back then was the John Lewis complex and pitch perimeter advertising boards," recalls Ken, "The club also had a lottery but that was running okay without any interference."

Left:
Demolition work starts on Nuttall Street

Top:
Bob Reynolds [Rovers' Lottery] pictured with Tony Parkes in 1977/78 at the launch of a new 10p lottery scheme at a local pub

Bottom:
Half time Lottery Draw with Jimmy Norris

92 Which former Arsenal legend scored on his Rovers debut against Oldham in February 1978?

(John Radford)

93 Name the goalkeeper Howard Kendall brought from non-league Stafford Rangers?

(Jim Arnold)

Little did Ken know, but the club - and the global game as a whole - was about to undergo something of a revolution.

Not that he wasn't prepared. Once his playing days were over a brief stint in management with Swindon convinced him that he needed another option.

He went into sales before spotting the Ewood position in the newspaper classifieds. Having never left the Blackburn area, even when transferred to Port Vale and then Tranmere, it was the ideal opportunity for Ken to get back into professional football.

Until that time, generating income in areas other than gate receipts was far less important than in today's highly commercialised game.

"As a Division Two club we knew we could only target local businesses for sponsorship and support. Direct mailing and phone calls drummed up surprising increases in trade but there was always a limit to how much we could achieve."

It was only in the late eighties that football experienced a boom.

Clubs started to realise that supplying kit or equipment had a commercial value. To have your company logo on the shirts of a team constantly challenging for promotion to the top flight of the Football League must carry both an attraction and a price.

The team set about negotiating kit deals and shirt sponsorship packages - a practice which became a popular marketing tool in the department's overall strategy.

"Being involved with sporting teams and events became all the rage and like everyone else it was essential that we cashed in."

One area staring Rovers in the face upon his arrival was the replica kit market.

Although shirts were available in the 80s, at Ewood they were stored in a cardboard box under the cash desk in the lottery shop - hardly the kind of merchandising which would prompt supporters to splash out.

Needless to say the situation was quickly remedied and the replica blue and white halves could soon be seen littered across the crowd of a Saturday afternoon.

Above:
Jack Walker celebrates from the Town Hall balcony

Below:
The open top bus

Having sported the club's trademark blue and white shirt himself, Ken is well aware of the euphoria brought about by the club's success. He was a key member of Rovers' 1974/75 third division-winning side contributing no less than 17 goals.

But the 1994/95 season enabled Rovers to experience a similar triumph from a different perspective.

Every living supporter will remember the tense weekend of May 13/14th 1995 when Rovers were crowned Premiership champions at Anfield.

But that was only the beginning for the team. From the moment the final whistle went with Rovers fans in ecstasy, the club's commercial team set about a mad 24-hour rush to present a celebration spectacular back at Ewood Park.

"To be involved in the arrangements for that special night was both a pleasure and a privilege," remembers Ken, "to turn the event around and accommodate a full house to welcome home the Premiership Champions inside 24 hours was very rewarding."

As a result of that magical weekend, Rovers gained entry to the European Champions League which spawned another commercial route for the club.

"We had an influx of people from a team management agency arrive at the club to ensure everything was being done by the UEFA book.

"From booking flights and hotels for our supporters to the organisation of corporate packages for our home ties and the advertising of our matches, it was great to be a part of it and it's something I'd love to be able to do again."

In the final few years of the 20th century, Rovers branched out via a business development department.

Now a sales team sources new forms of revenue, creating new opportunities.

The development of the Ewood Park Conference Centre has further diversified the club's commercial outlook.

These days everywhere from the Boardroom to the car park is available for hire to host events of almost any description.

Ken adds: "With the way the commercial side of the game has developed in recent years, it is quite unbelievable to think back to how things used to be not all that long ago."

One thing is for sure......the business of professional football will never again be simply about 22 men running around a field in search of goals and points.

Left:
The prestigious Boardroom

Right:
Premier Suite Ewood Park

94 Big defender who started with Ipswich and later played for Newcastle before turning in some sterling displays at Ewood Park. Name him

(Glenn Keeley)

The Business Story

Shopping Matters

Remember when football merchandise comprised of little more than scarves and bob hats, rosettes and rattles?

Pre-replica, pre-historic. Days, not all that long ago, when a guy stood against the outside wall of the Nuttall Street Stand flogging matchday programmes out of an old suitcase.

If someone back then asked you for directions for the "shop", chances are you would have pointed them the way of the chippie or the newsagents!

Not now though. The Club Shop is a focal point at every ground across the land - if football the game is big business then football merchandising is monster.

Rovers retailing has come a long way in a short time and there are few people better equipped to discuss it than Margaret Baldwin.

Margaret was there when it really started to kick off, around the mid-70s, and she remains a key member of the commercial department.

"Initially there wasn't what you would call a shop although we always felt there was a market for replica kit. What we didn't realise was how big a market.

"In 1975 Rovers' goods were housed in a corner of the old Co-op store in the town centre, and at one point we were selling things out of the lottery office and wherever else there was a bit of space. You could even buy a tie from the ticket office!

"I was working on the club lottery and we were a bit shocked when all of a sudden they told us we had to run a shop as well.

Basically we just knuckled down and got on with it. We even started to enjoy it - it was different and it was busy but it was fun!

"When a new kit came out, people queued up for what seemed like miles to get hold of one."

Jimmy Norris jumped on board in 1987. He remembers what it was like when Rovers first began to think seriously about merchandising.

"There was a time when we were working out of a tiny office without so much as a till. It was so small that if there were three people inside and one wanted to turn around the other two had to move!"

Left:
Picture taken around 1977/78 in the shop situated inside the local Co-op Store in Blackburn Town Centre

"It wasn't until we got to the Full Members Cup final in 1987 that merchandising really took off here. We had to sell things out of the back of a van because there was no room in the first shop. That was sited on Nuttall Street and you could only describe it as tiny.

"At one time there was just a small portakabin selling shirts and such like. Then came Nuttall Street before everything moved to the Blackburn End during the major ground development. Now we have a superb store - equal in size and lay-out to anything in town. How things change."

Duncan Martin has held the post of Rovers' Merchandising Manager for seven years, but his experience goes back much further. Working for thirteen years as a buyer for a Northern chain of sports shops, Duncan saw the commercial side of football grow at a phenomenal rate.

"It wasn't until the late 70s that club shops started to emerge," he remembers. "Even then it was very simple with only the most basic of items on sale.

"There was nothing much for children and ladies because it was really based on products that the players wore, like the shirts. But people were no longer satisfied with a few odds and ends and they started asking if we could supply more and more.

"I think it was the World Cup in 1982 that really sparked things off. Suddenly players were becoming recognised across the country rather than just by fans of their own team. Everyone knew Shilton, Robson and Lineker and the like. That's when we noticed a sudden upsurge in demand. People would come in asking if we had the Germany shirt or the Spain shirt, but of course nobody did because nobody had asked for them before."

Duncan recognises that summer as the turning point in football merchandising.

"It was the first time, for instance, that England produced souvenirs for the World Cup. After that it was quite a rapid progression to what you see today. It just exploded, everyone wanted to bring out the latest football merchandise."

That is how the Rovers' Club Shop became what it is today.

"We now carry around 2000 lines in total, and only 40% of our turnover comes from what would be called replica goods. You then have things like confectionery right down to telephones and CD players, it's quite diverse. We have also moved into things like ladies products and childrenswear, which gives us a whole new avenue to explore. A lot of people buy from us now who never come to the matches, whereas tracing back to the early days, that would never happen. It was just a case of 'I'm going to the game, I'll get a scarf', not any more."

At 42, Duncan has only been in the game a relatively short time, but he has seen quite a transformation.

95 Which Rovers defender was sold to Leeds to bring in a club record fee of £357,000 in 1979?

(Kevin Hird)

96 Which Wolves striker did Rovers sign in November 1981?

(Norman Bell)

"Most football clubs now are aware that there is a brand identity. You used to see a lot of people using the Blackburn Rovers name and logo on counterfeit goods, but that has changed as clubs and Trading Standards have dictated. Another thing is that the shop is not just part of the football club anymore, it is seen as a store in its own right selling a particular brand.

"When we built the current shop, "Rover the Moon," it was a straight business decision. We needed more floor space to supply the huge demand that there is now. We thought it would be easier for the customers if it was less cramped and a nicer working environment for the staff.

"That typifies the attitude towards the shop now, that it is part of the club but is a business in its own right as well. Having said that, the philosophy is that we can't sell products that are going to fall apart because it reflects badly on the club, and that will continue as long as we sell goods with the club crest on.

"It has always been a way of improving relations between the club and the fans because if we do sell things that fall apart, the fans who buy them feel that they are being taken advantage of by the club, but if the quality is good, they feel appreciated. That's important to Rovers, because we account for around 10% of the club's income."

Duncan hopes they have succeeded in pleasing the fans: "The most important thing for us has always been quality. If we think something is sub-standard we will pull it off the shelves and send it back. We always think about what we could do better so that the amount of money we take doesn't just depend on how well the team is doing, as it has in the past. We now try to sell more than just football related goods so that we can tell people they can buy a decent jacket or a pair of trainers at a fair price, so it doesn't matter whether the team won or lost. We are still as busy the week after a defeat as after a win, largely because fans prefer to support the team by giving their money to the club instead of a high street store. Obviously from a personal point of view we all feel down after a defeat, but professionally we must not let it affect us."

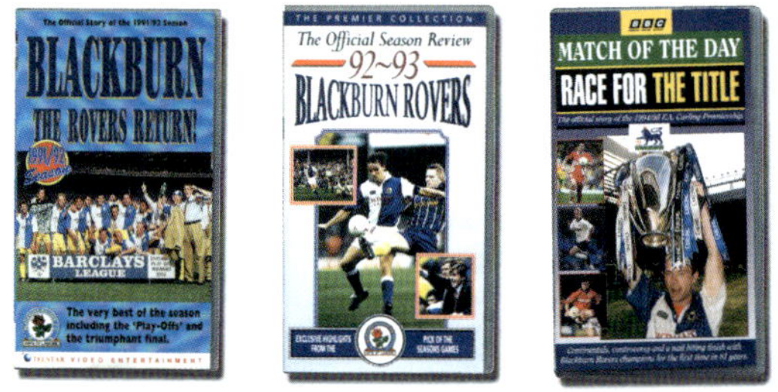

Far Left & Below:
Rover The Moon
Shop at Ewood Park

Left:
A selection of
Rovers' videos

Above:
Rovers' 'Directory'
[The brand new
merchandise catalogue
for 1999/2000]

That has led to other changes over the years, things which have changed the whole face of Ewood Park.

"The fans can now drive in and use the car parks whereas before they were walking a fair way just to get to the shop. Everything is nicely laid out in a real store instead of being behind a counter in a little office. We have tried to make it as comfortable as possible and it is more convenient for a lot of people than going into the town centre."

So what do the next 125 years hold....will the merchandising bubble continue to grow - or burst?

"Of course, every business needs to keep expanding, and not just in terms of size. Obviously there is a limit to how many shirts we can sell, so to grow we have to diversify again. Who knows what we could be doing next? Financial services, mortgages, rail travel, anything. People could ring up and say, "I'm a businessman, I'm a Rovers fan, I need to get to London, what can you do for me?" It's an extra sale to us but it's something they would have had to spend money on anyway. It's so different even from the seventies where it was a case of making sure we had enough scarves and bob-hats, which of course we still have to do! That's how the retail world is these days. When people go shopping they want to be able to go to one particular place and get more or less everything. That is what we are working towards."

97 Andy Crawford's only hat-trick for Rovers came against which club in April 1980?

(Reading)

PENDLE ANTIQUES CENTRE LTD.

Union Mill • Watt Street • Sabden • Lancashire BB7 9ED

Opening Times
Mon-Sat 10am-5pm
Sun 11am-5pm

Small Admission Fee
Adults 50p
Children 25p

Snacks and Refreshments Available

One of the largest selections of Pre-War Antiques, Furniture and Bric-a-Brac in the area, along with Architectural Items, Leaded Windows, Clocks and other various items.

International dealers stocking goods from both U.K. and overseas sources constantly changing with ten full-time dealers to maintain supplies and selection.

We urgently want to buy full or part house clearances, single items etc. Georgian Victorian, Edwardian, and later furniture, Bric-a-Brac, collectables, leaded stained glass windows and other architectural items. Discreet, confidential and courteous service.

To Sell Or Buy Goods - Telephone: 01282 776311

email: sales@pendleantiquescentre.co.uk

The Business Story

Every Picture Tells A Story

Left & Right: The beamback pictures from the 91/92 season play-offs at Derby

The Sports Pink will always have a warm place in the hearts of a certain generation of Rovers' fans.

Long ago, the Sports Pink and sister papers like the Football Post and the Green 'Un, were soccer gospels crammed full of essential facts and figures, news and reviews and on sale within an hour of the final whistle.

These days - with several notable exceptions - the late Saturday sports paper is a thing of the past, like celebrating two points for a win.

Football has changed a great deal over the years and will continue to change at a more accelerated rate over shorter periods of time.

Television - and Sky TV in particular - have changed the way we watch and the way we play the game. Depending on your point of view, or your age, you may think it is a good or a bad thing.

One thing is for sure - you will have an opinion about it.

Football has gone from a regional and quite domestic pastime with discussion, argument and opinion forming part of the social glue to a global, big money, new millennium sport that attracts TV, radio, internet and newspaper attention like bees around a honeypot.

But even that is changing and the focus of examination is becoming even more acute. Players are becoming higher paid, agents are more and more a significant part of the process, managers are sought-after TV pundits and fans are becoming more and more vocal.

Complimenting all that, video technology has come of age and with the promise of broadband, digital and interactive services we will all have more to watch...and hopefully, more to enjoy.

But despite all these technical advances we must not lose sight of our original motives - a shared love of football, for a game that disappoints as much as it pleases.

98 Who was Rovers chairman between 1982 and 1991?

(William Fox)

99 Against which club did Rovers secure promotion to Division Two in 1980 with a 2-1 win?

(Bury)

Football is the most significant shared experience in today's society. Even Coronation Street or EastEnders cannot match in a year the variety of plots and stories that appear spontaneously in a single week throughout football.

It is magnetic, which is why we all love our clubs.

It is also why from time to time we hate our clubs and our teams. Football is part of the family and we all argue with family, don't we?

In this highly-charged environment, with media hype, Blackburn Rovers have an even more difficult job in delivering messages into an increasingly crowded marketplace.

Right:
Publishing with Roar

Below Right:
Hard at work in the gallery

Left:
David on Camera

To continue to succeed as a big club and as an important player in the business of football is an integral part of Rovers' future plans.

Blackburn Rovers has been at the forefront of helping make this a reality through the media - our media.

Radio Rovers was our first excursion into broadcasting, it went on air on October 31st 1993. The concept itself was unique in that Rovers was the first football club ever to be granted a radio broadcast licence.

In 1998, the club took a massive forward step by investing £2.5m in a state-of-the-art Media Suite, complete with an in-house match-day television station, RoverVision.

100 From which club did Rovers procure manager Bob Saxton in 1981?

(Plymouth)

101 How much did Rovers pay for goalkeeper Terry Gennoe £50,000, £60,000 or £70,000?

(£60,000)

A fully digital broadcast quality production facility with on-line and off-line editing, digital effects and graphics. It even has its own self-contained studio that any national television company would be proud to call its own.

The Media Centre gives the club an opportunity to say what it wants to say in the way we want to say it at the time of our choosing. We are also focusing on improving the products we sell to you.

Right:
The purpose built state-of-the-art television studio

RoverTime is a good example: major improvements across the board in terms of content, design and photography.

There is a new and expanding Web Site (and the ability to build others) and a publishing business.

The overall aim is to use these abilities and facilities to grow the club's public image and produce an income stream to contribute to the general income. Club videos are now produced in-house within our publishing department.

Additionally, the Media Centre has worked with - and for - a number of external clients in producing corporate video, brochures and advertising.

In all of this, Blackburn Rovers truly is in a league of its own.

The Business Story

Rover 'n' Out . . . And About!

Football in the community.

Surely, twas ever thus? Not quite.

It may always have been the community's game, the game both "for" and "in" the community - but never like this.

For Community now add Department - a seven-day operation and a major part of soccer life, nowhere more so than at Ewood Park.

Peter Devine has been the Blackburn Rovers Community Officer for the past 11 years. In that time he has seen the organisation's involvement in the local - and not so local - area grow at an astonishing rate.

"To start with there was very little happening here. Like anything else the project started out small."

But it wasn't to stay that way. Growth has been rapid.

"We kicked off in a terraced house close to the ground, but as the club began to grow, so did we. As soon as the Brockhall training ground was up and running we moved into the indoor centre and from there we began expanding into things like the soccer schools.

"Now schools can book us to go in once a week, free of charge, for six weeks.

We get to know the kids as players, point out where they are going wrong and hopefully make them better footballers. Obviously the main thing is that they have a good time and enjoy themselves.
We get immense satisfaction in helping them progress.

"If the schools want us to go in after school time then there is a charge for each child, but the money is split between us and the school. That way the school makes money while our share is re-invested in the community scheme, so everyone wins."

The work doesn't stop there. There are plenty of other activities to keep the staff busy.

"Birthday parties are the most rewarding activity for the staff because the kids have such a good time you can't help but go home feeling happy with the job you've done! Basically they get to go on a ground tour before going down to the indoor centre for a game of football.

102 Which Rovers striker was brought down for the penalty which Mike Newell converted to earn Rovers promotion in the 1992 play-off final?

(David Speedie)

"The birthday boy or girl gets an autographed football, and for an extra charge they can even have the mascot, Roar, attend the party, which brings something a bit special to the day because the kids love him! At the end of the day we all go up to McDonald's for a meal at a reduced cost. The feedback from the parties has been very encouraging, even though we get a few grazed knees from the football games. Youngsters are very competitive!

"On matchdays we run what we call Saturday Clubs. Every home game that the team has we are given a certain amount of tickets which are used to try and get youngsters involved in Blackburn Rovers. Sometimes we get individuals making up a group or, as is more and more the case nowadays, junior football teams come for a day out.

"They can come and watch the games, have an hour's coaching, play in a mini-tournament and have something to eat at McDonald's, so it is a good day out. If anyone brings down ten or more kids they get an autographed football to boot. That has been quite successful but even that isn't as big as the soccer schools.

"Every school holiday we run the schools for all age groups from five years up to sixteen year-olds. It started just in the local area but as word got around and the demand for them grew, and now we've started going as far as Cumbria, Newcastle, even Scotland. The furthest we've travelled was when we went to Gutersloh army barracks in Germany for a five day coaching course. I don't think the staff were too keen to point out the footballing weaknesses of 15 stone, shaven-headed men who play with guns all day, but it was still quite successful!

"A few years back we started running the indoor football leagues. They have taken off in a big way. We have company leagues, veterans leagues and open leagues, Sundays and midweek, and they have proved to be a huge success.

"The leagues are mainly for adults but that just gives the older members of the community a way to get involved with the club. There is a cup competition for each league and at the end of the season there is a very entertaining presentation evening in one of the suites at Ewood Park. Again, it is all done for a small cost which just covers expenses."

So where does the project go from here? "We are now trying to get more involved with things like Asian football, Ladies football, work with the elderly and the disabled, any way at all we can help the community and at the same time raise the profile of the club.

"That is the main point behind it all, to raise awareness of Blackburn Rovers FC and put something back into the community. The people of Blackburn do a lot for the club and this is the club's way of repaying them. That is why we try to keep the cost to a minimum.

"This is just an honest thank-you gesture, not just to the fans who come here every week but to the people of Blackburn who have helped make the club what it is today."

Above and previous page:
BRFC mascots
Roar and Roarina

103 In what year did Alan Shearer sign for Rovers?

(1992)

104 What was the score in Rovers' last home Premiership game against Manchester United in May 1999?

(0-0)

The Business Story

Making A Meal Of It

ewood express

Catering by Blackburn Rovers

The face of the English game is changing, at every level. In front of and behind the scenes, our national game is increasingly a global concern.

At such a volatile time, the honest, down-to-earth football supporter needs to cling on to the grass roots as he faces the future with some trepidation.

Pies give him that opportunity.

Nothing holds off the icy chill of a winter gale better than a meat and potato pie special, just ask any of the Ewood Park regulars who manage to chomp their way through an average of over 3,000 pies and pasties every home game.

Rovers' Catering Manager Janet Jenkin fully understands the role of the pie within football which is why, within months of her arrival in February 1999, the club took over full catering for Ewood concourses, installing 33 brand new ovens into the bargain.

Janet, who previously worked at Granada Studios, Camelot and the Brighton Conference Centre, has the responsibility of keeping all the stadium catering outlets fully stocked and running like clockwork.

"A pie and a pint are still the two most popular items sold on matchdays," says Janet. "But people do request other food and so we have introduced new varieties including a vegetarian option last year which quickly caught on. We've also started selling pizzas and chicken nuggets."

But pies are still number one. Of course they are.

"Football food has to be hand to mouth, and pies are ideal. Ewood houses 16 food outlets and 17 beer kiosks also selling pies."

But pies are by no means the only form of catering on the menu.

Increasingly over the last few years a new breed of football fan has emerged and corporate hospitality now represents a huge part of match-day proceedings and a vital source of extra revenue.

Hundreds of pre-match guests now enjoy either a five-course sit-down meal or a running buffet ahead of kick-off while innovative packages including match and ball sponsorship and the like have become ever more popular amid the soccer revolution.

The club aims to attract business users, not just on match-days, to the extensive facilities within the various function rooms and the newly-christened Ewood Park Conference Centre.

blues
café bar

Above:
The blues café bar

Top Right:
The Premier Suite

Bottom Right:
The Directors' lounge

The Centre has enjoyed a significant increase in turnover. Rovers have taken a very pro-active approach to publicising the Centre and are justly proud of the rooms, facilities and levels of food and service on offer.

The club caters for everyone from a pre-match table for four or a full-scale dinner for up to 300 guests.

105 Who did Rovers beat 7-0 in November 1995?

(Nottingham Forest)

106 Against which club did Chris Sutton score his first Rovers goal in August 1994?

(Coventry City)

107 Who took over from Don MacKay as Rovers' manager in 1991?

(Kenny Dalglish)

The Business Story

Ground Force

The road to Ewood Park was not particularly long, but it was certainly winding.

From the Oozehead Ground in 1876 to Pleasington in 1877, Alexandra Meadows a year later and Leamington Road for a nine-year stint.

Ewood Park did not become a permanent fixture until 1890.

Originally built by four Blackburn tradesmen, Ewood Park became Rovers' new base when the owner of the Leamington Road ground hiked up the rent.

At first, football took a back seat to dog racing and athletics - but not for long!

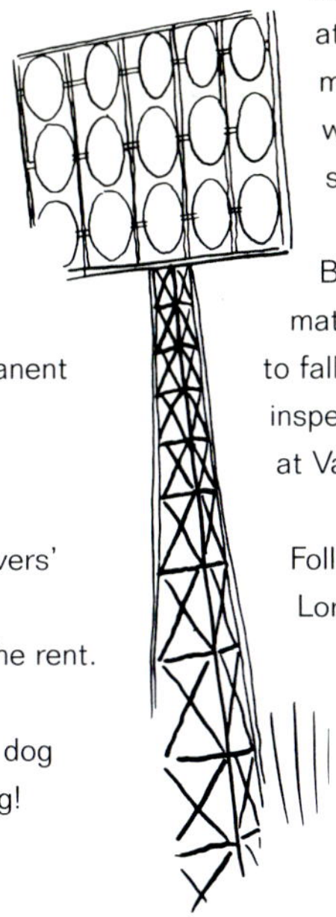

Ewood Park was always considered one of England's best - a fine old ground, steeped in tradition; a ground of atmosphere, crammed with memories - the sort of place where you could hear the fans singing even on non-match days!

But old wooden structures, no matter how historic or noble, were to fall foul of the nation's safety inspectors after two major disasters - at Valley Parade and Hillsborough.

Following the Hillsborough tragedy, Lord Justice Taylor made a number of recommendations. He wanted to get everyone to sit down for matches and for clubs to introduce sophisticated safety features.

Left:
Aerial view of the stadium 1928

Rovers may have been in the old Second Division at that time, but the club was committed to achieving a top flight goal 'inside two years'.

Think ahead and think big was the message as Rovers officials, led by current Chairman Robert Coar, set about the task of shaping the way forward.

Everything seemed to change overnight on a truly massive scale although, much to the delight and relief of the fans, those in charge opted against changing the address.

The bulldozers moved in and under the enthusiastic and expert leadership of Mr Coar and his team a new Ewood emerged - a ground immediately acclaimed as one of the most attractive, advanced and safest in Europe....inside and out.

Fans found greater levels of match-day comfort while business clients discovered unrivalled corporate facilities.
And not only did it look well - it worked well too.

108 Who took over from Kenny Dalglish as Rovers manager in 1995?

(Ray Harford)

109 Name the midfielder signed from West Ham in the summer of 1995 who later returned to London?

(Matty Holmes)

Top Left:
Another aerial view of the stadium

Top Right:
Demolition begins at the Blackburn End

Bottom:
Dramatic scenes when the big machines move in

John Newsham, later to be appointed Safety Officer, started as a steward while the scaffolding was still in place. He was one of 83 back then - these days there are 400 stewards on the books, with an average 320 on any one game.

"The changes here over the last 10 years have been truly phenomenal," says John.

"The old stadium control room used to be in the groundsman's hut and consisted of a couple of monitors, eight radios - not all of them working - and a PA system!

"During the re-developments the control room switched to a Portakabin for a couple of seasons, but when the Blackburn End incorporated the current hi-tech set-up it was like moving into Cape Canaveral!

"The equipment we have in there is the best in the field and we still have clubs from both home and abroad coming to see how we run things, but we have never rested on our laurels and have upgraded our equipment at every available opportunity.

This Page: Different stages of development at Ewood Park

110 From which club did Rovers sign Jeff Kenna in 1995?

(Southampton)

111 Against who did Rovers winger Stuart Ripley win his first England cap in 1993?

(San Marino)

112 Which defender won a Premier League runners up medal with Rovers in 1994 and then again with Manchester United in 1995?

(David May)

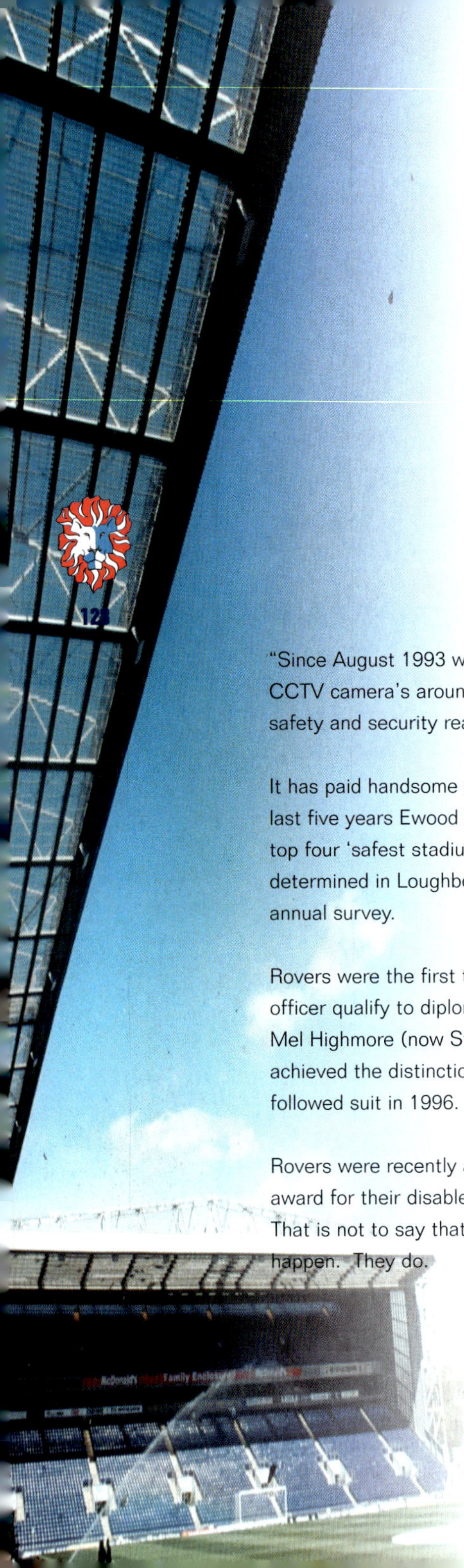

A Celebration of 125 Years of Blackburn Rovers
Our Goals Are Yours

Left:
Panoramic of the new Ewood Park stadium

Above:
Detail from commemorative plaque

"Since August 1993 we have built up 15 CCTV camera's around the ground for both safety and security reasons."

It has paid handsome dividends. During the last five years Ewood Park has been in the top four 'safest stadiums' in the country, as determined in Loughborough University's annual survey.

Rovers were the first to have a safety officer qualify to diploma level when Mel Highmore (now Stadium Manager) achieved the distinction in 1994. John followed suit in 1996.

Rovers were recently awarded a national award for their disabled facilities.
That is not to say that accidents no longer happen. They do.

"We have reduced the number of reported injuries by 50 per cent," adds John.
"When we had terracing the most common were twisted or broken ankles, probably from supporters landing badly after Rovers scored!

"Since we went all-seater the most common injury involves fingers, people trap them in the flip-up seats and we have also seen an increase in wasp stings because people can no longer beat a hasty retreat!"

DATELINE

1875	All games played away
1876	Oozehead Ground
1877	Pleasington
1878	Alexandra Meadows
1881	Leamington Road
1890	Ewood Park - ten year lease
1893	Bought ground for £2,500
1905	12,000 capacity covered Darwen End Stand built for £1,680
1906	Nuttall Street Stand built, opened New Years Day against PNE
1913	Riverside Stand built
1915	Ewood Park capacity around 71,000
1958	Floodlights
1960	Covered Blackburn End (all four sides covered)
1984	Fire in Nuttall Street Stand
1987	Riverside Stand demolished due to crumbling foundations and re-built
1989	Innovative undersoil heating on pitch, first club in country to experiment with it
1990	New electronic scoreboard
1992/93	Darwen End and Blackburn End demolished and rebuilt
1993/94	Nuttall Street Stand demolished and rebuilt as Jack Walker Stand

113 Which Rovers star was sent off in the 1994 Premier League clash with Manchester United at Ewood Park?

(Henning Berg)

21st Century Stories

21st Century Stories

The Academy

It took the collective efforts of seventeen academics to get Blackburn Rovers FC up and running 125 years ago..and, much later, the fanatical involvement of one local-boy-made-very-good to take it to the pinnacle of its achievement.

But while the original founders, graduates from Blackburn Grammar School led by John Lewis, are now visible only through their legacy; Jack Walker, the man who guided the club to unprecedented glory, continues very much at the forefront.

He remains a man with both a passion and a vision; a man determined to lay the foundations upon which to take the club into 2000 and beyond.

The mainstay of those foundations opened just weeks before the dawn of the new Millennium..The Academy - a multi-million pound, futuristic training facility which highlights exactly why Rovers are rated pioneers in the British youth football revolution.

Left:
The Academy main entrance

Above:
Hydrotherapy pool

Right:
The Academy dining area

Within half-a-mile of the senior training headquarters at Brockhall, the space-age Academy is cloaked in the club's trademark blue and white halves to combine forward thinking and the proud Ewood tradition.

The 20-acre complex incorporates five full-size outdoor pitches to accommodate training and competitive matches for no fewer than ten youth teams aged from eight years upwards. There is a huge indoor arena - incorporating a half-size artificial pitch and a four-lane sprint track - which allows training to go ahead whatever the weather.

Top:
Physiotherapy room

Bottom:
The impressive indoor pitch (80yds x 50yds)

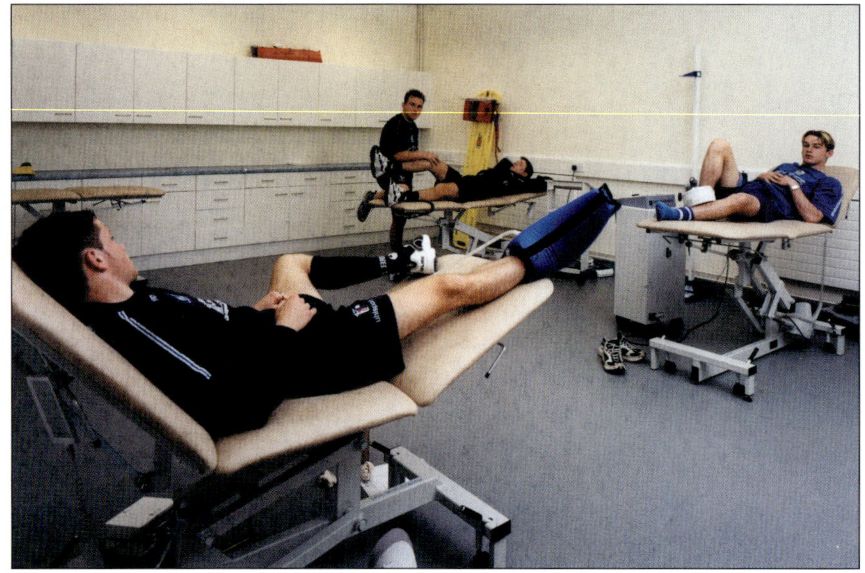

The facility has seven changing rooms, a fully-equipped medical treatment room plus laundry, kitchen and dining facilities, not to mention a high-tech gymnasium, administration offices, conference rooms and a spacious players' lounge plus a custom-built swimming pool and steam room.

What also makes Rovers' Academy stand out from the crowd is a superb on-site lodge, designed to accommodate up to 32 boys (two full squads) plus supervisors and houseparents. This enables the club to monitor every aspect of their young player's development from diet to training to recreation.

The Academy made a flying start to life under the new regime by winning the FA Premier Academy League Under 17s title in the inaugural season.

Rovers hope The Academy will produce a conveyor belt of soccer talent and, once again everyone associated with Blackburn Rovers is indebted to the foresight and support of Jack Walker for turning a dream into reality.

114 Which Premier League club held Manchester United to a draw in 1995, handing Rovers the championship?
(West Ham United)

115 Against which club did Kevin Gallacher score and break his leg in the same game in 1995?
(Crystal Palace)

116 A former Young boy of Berne who left Rovers to become a Ram. Name him?
(Lars Bohinen)

117 Who in the 1990s went from being a Saint to a Rover and then became a Fox?
(Tim Flowers)

21st Century Stories

The Way Forward

It is difficult to visualise just what challenges will confront professional football over the coming years.

But rest assured that whatever those challenges and changes are, they will be both significant and far reaching.

Many believe it inevitable that further re-structuring and streamlining at the top end of the pyramid will simply lead to the rich getting richer and the poor getting poorer.

Assuming that forecast to be accurate, it is imperative that Blackburn Rovers seize every opportunity to ensure a place among the top bracket over the long term.

To achieve this goal we must look the hard facts straight between the eyes and a key word in our future has got to be - diversification.

No longer can the majority of football clubs pay their way through the traditional income stream of cash at the turnstile.

Left: Media development of an animated cartoon series. 'The Likeaballs' are already a regular feature in Rovertime

Gate receipts no longer meet running costs.

The two factors likely to have most influence on what happens in the short and medium term future are television rights and players' wages. The introduction of digital television already presents more income options, but the continuing impact of Bosman brings ever spiralling salaries.

So it will be through other sources of revenue that we look to develop our business.

A couple of years ago the Ewood Park hierarchy, under the guidance of Jack Walker and Robert Coar, decided to explore all available avenues.

Right: BRFC joined forces with dedicated Blackburn fan, Wayne Hemingway of Red or Dead to produce a range of clothing based on Rovers' First Team strip - available in Rover the Moon

They appointed John Williams, a man with a wealth of business experience, as the club's first Chief Executive and recruited a leading football administrator as Secretary (Tom Finn).

118 James Edward are the middle names of which former Rovers defensive who had two highly-successful spells before going north of the border?

(Colin Hendry)

119 Which former Ewood striker scored against Rovers in April 1999 for the Saints?

(James Beattie)

A Celebration of 125 Years of Blackburn Rovers
Our Goals Are Yours

DRUMHAWK
COMMUNICATIONS

Both men, who also sit on the Board, are convinced that the key to a bright future on the field lies on how successful a club can be off it.

"We must maximise the potential of our commercial activities," says Mr Williams. "Running a top football club is a big-money exercise these days, and nothing suggests that will change. If anything it will get even more costly for it is unlikely that we will ever see any collective cap on wages being imposed.

"So, if you want to compete alongside the best clubs and attempt to attract and keep a hold of the best players you must have a very strong financial base.

"Over recent months we have taken further steps to that end. We have established under our umbrella a new agency, Drumhawk Communications, which offers business clients a full range of media services to encompass print, publicity, advertising, television, video and Internet.

"Our aim is to be at the cutting edge, leading the charge rather than scampering along in breathless pursuit.

"We always endeavour to look further than the present when we make a commercial move - take our state-of-the-art Media Centre, the arrival of RoverVision and the impressive new Rover the Moon retail store.

"But in all of this we must not forget our fans. We must pursue honest and open commercial policies that correctly balance and value the needs of the club and its customers.

"Now we plan to give our supporters and our customers the best Internet service possible as we try to keep pace with rapid developments in technology.

"All areas of our commercial business come under constant scrutiny. To stand still is to drift backwards.

Bottom Left: Merchandising diversity inside Rover the Moon

Above Left & Right: Samples of the BRFC/Red or Dead collection available from Rover the Moon

120 Name the striker Rovers signed from Roma during Roy Hodgson's reign as manager?

(Martin Dahlin)

121 Against who did Kevin Davies score his first Rovers league goal?

¿! (Charlton)

"Traditional income avenues like match-day sponsorships and lotteries remain very important, but there are so many other areas available to us now and we cannot afford to pass up on a single one.

"All of this will help us to achieve our overall objective of establishing Blackburn Rovers as a recognised force in football and maintain our reputation as a community club."

Left:
Rover The Moon at Ewood Park Blackburn

Above:
Samples of the BRFC/Red or Dead collection available from Rover the Moon

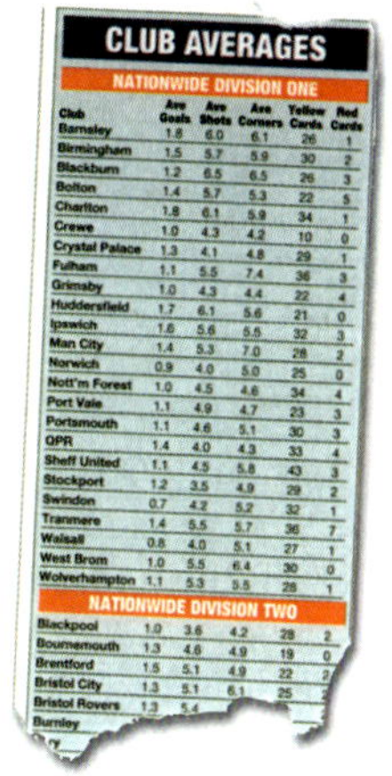

CLUB AVERAGES

Club	Ave Goals	Ave Shots	Ave Corners	Yellow Cards	Red Cards
NATIONWIDE DIVISION ONE					
Barnsley	1.8	6.0	6.1	26	1
Birmingham	1.5	5.7	5.9	30	2
Blackburn	1.2	6.5	6.5	26	3
Bolton	1.4	5.7	5.3	22	5
Charlton	1.8	6.1	5.9	34	1
Crewe	1.0	4.3	4.2	10	0
Crystal Palace	1.3	4.1	4.8	29	1
Fulham	1.1	5.5	7.4	36	3
Grimsby	1.0	4.3	4.4	22	4
Huddersfield	1.7	6.1	5.6	21	0
Ipswich	1.6	5.6	5.5	32	3
Man City	1.4	5.3	7.0	28	2
Norwich	0.9	4.0	5.0	25	0
Nott'm Forest	1.0	4.5	4.6	34	4
Port Vale	1.1	4.9	4.7	23	3
Portsmouth	1.1	4.6	5.1	30	3
QPR	1.4	4.0	4.3	33	4
Sheff United	1.1	4.5	5.8	43	3
Stockport	1.2	3.5	4.9	29	2
Swindon	0.7	4.2	5.2	32	1
Tranmere	1.4	5.5	5.7	36	7
Walsall	0.8	4.0	5.1	27	1
West Brom	1.0	5.5	6.4	30	0
Wolverhampton	1.1	5.3	5.5	28	1
NATIONWIDE DIVISION TWO					
Blackpool	1.0	3.6	4.2	28	2
Bournemouth	1.3	4.6	4.9	19	0
Brentford	1.5	5.1	4.9	22	2
Bristol City	1.3	5.1	6.1	25	[illegible]
Bristol Rovers	1.3	5.4	[illegible]	[illegible]	[illegible]
Burnley	[illegible]	[illegible]	[illegible]	[illegible]	[illegible]

The Numbers Game

The Numbers Game

Dream Team

Stats man Derek Jones has been keeping Rovers' records ever since attending his first Ewood match as a youngster on Christmas Day, 1951.

Here he nominates five teams of the decade in 4-4-2 formation, covering the period he has followed the club. No doubt his overall choice will provoke some debate, but Derek reckons the back four picks itself!

He rates Bryan Douglas the most skilful player he has seen in a Rovers' shirt and, the Championship apart, his greatest thrill was watching boyhood idol Tommy Briggs score seven goals in one afternoon.

BEST OF THE FIVE DECADES

Tim Flowers

Keith Newton
Colin Hendry
Mike England
Bill Eckersley

Bryan Douglas
Ronnie Clayton
Roy Vernon
Bobby Langton

Simon Garner
Alan Shearer

Subs:
Roger Jones (g)
Derek Fazackerley
Tim Sherwood
Andy McEvoy
Tommy Briggs

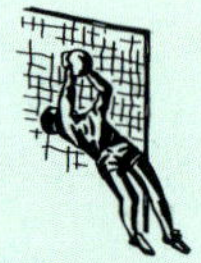

Goalkeeper
50s – Reg Elvy
60s – Fred Else
70s – Roger Jones
80s – Terry Gennoe
90s – Tim Flowers

Defence
50s – Ron Suart
60s – Keith Newton
70s – Kevin Hird
80s – Jim Branagan
90s – Henning Berg

Defence
50s – Matt Woods
60s – Alan Hunter
70s – Graham Hawkins
80s – Glenn Keeley
90s – Stephane Henchoz

Defence
50s – Willie Kelly
60s – Mike England
70s – Derek Fazackerley
80s – Derek Fazackerley
90s – Colin Hendry

Defence
50s – Bill Eckersley
60s – Billy Wilson
70s – John Bailey
80s – Mick Rathbone
90s – Graeme Le Saux

Midfield
50s – Bryan Douglas
60s – Mike Ferguson
70s – Ken Beamish
80s – Noel Brotherston
90s – Stuart Ripley

Midfield
50s – Ronnie Clayton
60s – Ronnie Clayton
70s – Stuart Metcalfe
80s – Simon Barker
90s – Tim Sherwood

Midfield
50s – Roy Vernon
60s – Bryan Douglas
70s – Tony Parkes
80s – Nicky Reid
90s – Mark Atkins

Midfield
50s – Bobby Langton
60s – Mike Harrison
70s – Dave Wagstaffe
80s – Scott Sellars
90s – Jason Wilcox

Striker
50s – Peter Dobing
60s – Andy McEvoy
70s – Don Martin
80s – Simon Garner
90s – Alan Shearer

Striker
50s – Tommy Briggs
60s – Fred Pickering
70s – Tony Field
80s – Howard Gayle
90s – Chris Sutton

122 Who was Brian Kidd's first signing as Rovers manager?

(Keith Gillespie)

123 Who scored Rovers' two goals in the 3-2 defeat at Manchester United in 1998-99?

(Dario Marcolin and Nathan Blake)

Current Senior Officials

Jack Walker

Robert D Coar

Richard L Matthewman

Senior Vice President
Jack Walker

Club President
William H Bancroft

Chairman
Robert D Coar BSc

Vice Chairman
Richard L Matthewman

Chief Executive
John O Williams BSc

Secretary
Tom Finn MBA

Directors
Keith C Lee
Iain R Stanners
George R Root FCMA
Tom Finn MBA
John O Williams BSc

Vice Presidents
Edgar Pickering
Dr Milton Jeffries TD

John O Williams

Tom Finn

William H Bancroft

George R Root

Iain R Stanners

Keith C Lee

Edgar Pickering

Dr Milton Jeffries

Managers

Before Jack Carr became the club's first manager in 1922, team matters were in the hands of a committee, usually comprising the secretary, Head Trainer and Directors. Eddie Quigley, Richard Dinnis, John Pickering, Norman Bodell and Tony Parkes (five times) have all held the position of caretaker-manager until a permanent appointment was made.

Jack Carr: February, 1922 - December, 1926
Bob Crompton: December, 1926 - February, 1931
Arthur Barritt: February 1931 - March, 1936
Reg Taylor: October, 1936 - May, 1938
Bob Crompton: May, 1938 - March, 1941
Eddie Hapgood: January, 1946 - February, 1947
Will Scott: May - December, 1947
Jack Bruton: December, 1947 - May, 1949
Jack Bestall: June, 1949 - May, 1953
Johnny Carey: August, 1953 - October, 1958
Dally Duncan: October, 1958 - June, 1960
Jack Marshall: September, 1960 - February, 1967
Eddie Quigley: April, 1967 - October, 1970
Johnny Carey: October, 1970 - June, 1971
Ken Furphy: July, 1971 - December, 1973
Gordon Lee: January, 1974 - June, 1975
Jim Smith: June, 1975 - March, 1978
Jim Iley: April - October, 1978
John Pickering: February - May, 1979
Howard Kendall: (player-manager): June, 1979 - May, 1981
Bob Saxton: June, 1981 - December, 1986
Don MacKay: February, 1987 - September, 1991
Kenny Dalglish: October, 1991 - June, 1995
Ray Harford: June, 1995 - October, 1996
Roy Hodgson: July, 1997 - November, 1998
Brian Kidd: December, 1998 - November 1999
Tony Parkes: December 1999 -

Chairmen

1875-1888	Lewis J
1888-1901	Morley E S
1901-1905	Birtwistle R
1905-1919	Cotton L
1919-1921	Cotton C
1921-1933	Walsh JW
1933-1938	Tempest W
1938-1943	Cotton J
1944-1948	Caton J
1948- 1952	Wood F
1952-1956	Blackshaw T
1956-1960	Forbes G N
1960-1964	Wilkinson J
1964-1968	Hull D
1968-1970	Davies C R
1970-1971	Fryars A L
1971-1979	Bancroft W H
1979	Keighley D T
1979-1982	Brown D
1982-1991	Fox W
1991-	Coar R D

The Numbers Game

Full International Caps Gained by Rovers' Players

Goals scored in brackets. *Additional caps with other club(s). As at July 1999.

England:

Arthur, JWH 7
Barton, J 1 (1)
Batty, D 3*
Beverley, J 3
Blackburn, F 3 (1)
Booth, TE 1*
Bradshaw, W 4
Brown, J 5 (3)
Campbell, AF 2*
Chippendale, H 1
Clayton, R 35
Cowell, A 1
Crompton, R 41
Cunliffe, A 2
Douglas, B 36 (11)
Eckersley, W 17
Flowers, TD 10*
Forrest, JH 11
Greenwood, DH 2
Hargreaves, FW 3
Hargreaves, J 2
Harper, EC 1
Healless, H 2
Hodkinson, J 3
Houlker, AE 1*
Jones, H 6
Langton, R 7 (1)*
Latheron, EG 2 (1)
Le Saux, GP 20 (1)*
Lofthouse, JM 6 (2)*
Newton, KR 19*
Puddefoot, SC 2
Rigby, A 5 (3)
Ripley, SE 2
Sewell, WR 1
Shea, D 2
Shearer, A 25 (9)*
Simpson, J 8 (1)
Southworth,John 3 (3)
Sutton, CR 1
Townley, WJ 2 (2)
Walton, N 1
Whitehead, J 1*
Wilcox, JM 2
Wolstenholme, S 2*

Scotland:

Aitkenhead, WAC 1 (2)
Brandon, T1
Dailly, CE 1*
Davidson, CI 7
Gallacher, KW 29 (8)*
Hendry, ECJ 35 (1)*
Hutton, J 3*
McKay, J 1
McKinlay, WJA 15*

Wales:

Blake, NA 1*
Coleman, C 5*
Davies, W 9 (5)*
England, HM 20 (1)*
Evans, RO 1*
Hole, BG 7*
Hughes, JI 1
Hughes, WA 5
Oliver, A 1*
Vernon, TR 9 (1)*

Ireland/N Ireland:

Brotherston, N 27 (3)
Crossan, E 3 (1)
Dougan, AD 5 (2)*
Fettis, AW 7*
Gillespie, KR 2*
Hunter, A 6*
Johnson, DM 1
Lawther, WI 2*
Quinn, JM 13 (3)*
Robinson, P 1*
Rollo, D 12*

Republic of Ireland:

Carsley, LK 2*
Duff, DA 9
Given, SJJ 9*
Haverty, J 2*
Kenna, JJ 26
McAteer, JW 2*
McEvoy MA 17 (6)
McGrath, M 18*
Moran, KB 24*
Rogers, E 14 (3)*
Stapleton, FA 2 (2)*

Denmark:

Pedersen, PW 3 (1)*

Greece:

Donis, G 7 (1)*

Norway:

Berg, H 37 (4)*
Bohinen, L 4*

Sweden:

Andersson, AP 1*
Andersson, PJ 7*
Dahlin, M 4*

Switzerland:

Henchoz, S 14*

USA:

Wegerle, RC 4 (1)*

124 True or false - Rovers never once held a top ten position during their Premiership relegation season?

(True)

125 Who scored Rovers last Premiership goal at Newcastle in 1999?

(Jason Wilcox)

The Numbers Game

Club Records

Record win:
11-0 v Rossendale United, home,
FA Cup First Round, October 13, 1884.

Record League win:
9-0 v Middlesbrough, home,
Div 2, November 6, 1954.

Record away League win:
8-2 v West Ham United,
Div 1, December 26, 1963.

Record League defeat:
0-8 v Arsenal, away, Div 1, February 25, 1933;
v Lincoln City, away Div 2, August 29, 1953.

Record home League defeat:
1-7 v Notts County, March 14, 1891; v Middlesbrough,
Div 1, November 29, 1947.

Record aggregate League score:
5-8 v Derby County, away,
September 6, 1890.

Record aggregate home League score:
7-5 v Birmingham City, Div 1, September 28, 1929.

Most League appearances:
Derek Fazackerley, 593+3s, 1970-71 to 1986-87.

Most International appearances:
Bob Crompton, England, 41, 1901-02 to 1913-14.

Most individual League goals-
In a match: Tommy Briggs, 7 v Bristol Rovers, home,
Div 2, February 5, 1955.
In a season: Ted Harper, 43, Div 1, 1925-26.
In aggregate: Simon Garner, 168, 1978-79 to 1991-92.

Most consecutive League appearances:
Walter Crook, 208.

Most League appearances by a goalkeeper:
Terry Gennoe, 289, 1981-82 to 1990-91.

Most consecutive League appearances by a goalkeeper:
Reg Elvy, 152.

Most clean sheets by a goalkeeper in a League season:
19, Jim Arnold, Div 3, 1979-80;
Bobby Mimms, Prem Lge, 1992-93.

Most collective clean sheets in a League season:
23, Div 2, 1980-81.

Most hat-tricks in a season:
8, 1963-64.

Most individual hat-tricks -
In a season: 5, John Southworth (1890-91);
Andy McEvoy (1963-64), Alan Shearer (1995-96).
In aggregate: 13, John Southworth.

Most League appearances as a substitute -
In a season: 17, Lenny Johnrose, 1990-91.
In aggregate: 29, Simon Garner.

First substitution:
John Byrom (for Mick McGrath, injured),
v Manchester United, away, Div 1, November 6, 1965.

Youngest player:
Harry Dennison, aged 16 years, 155 days
(v Bristol City, home, Div 1, April 8, 1911).

Oldest player:
Bob Crompton, aged 40 years, 150 days
(v Bradford Park Avenue, away, Div 1, February 23, 1920.)

Most penalties converted by one player:
In a season: 10, Alan Shearer, 1994-95.
In aggregate: 22, Billy Bradshaw

Most players used in a season:
39, 1919-20.

Most goalkeepers used in a season:
6, 1889-90.

Fewest players used in a season:
17, 1985-86.

Most FA Cup appearances:
56, Ronnie Clayton.

Most League Cup appearances:
38, Derek Fazackerley.

Most FA Cup goals: -
In a match: 4, James Brown (1882-83, 1883-84);
Herbert Fecitt (1884-85); John Southworth (1888-89, 1891-92).
In a season: 9, Herbert Fecitt, 1884-85.
In aggregate: 29, James Brown.

Most League Cup goals -
In a match: 4, Eddie Thomas, v Bristol Rovers, home,
Second Round Replay, October 16, 1961.
In a season: 6, Alan Shearer, 1992-93.
In aggregate: 14, Alan Shearer.

Most FA Cup Winners' medals:
5, James Forrest, 1884, 1885, 1886, 1890, 1891
(equals FA Cup record).

Record attendance:
61,783 v Bolton Wanderers, FA Cup Sixth Round, March 2 1929.

Record receipts:
£333,067 v Liverpool, League Cup Fourth Round,
November 30, 1994.

Highest League attendance:
52,656 v Preston North End, Div 1, December 26, 1921.

Lowest League attendance:
3,107 v Cardiff City, Div 2, May 7, 1984.

Lowest Cup attendance:
2,161 v Wimbledon, League Cup,
Second Round (2nd Leg), October 8, 1985.

Record Transfer Fees -
Paid: £7,250,000 for Kevin Davies (Southampton), June 1998.
Received: £15,000,000 for Alan Shearer
(Newcastle United), July 1996.

Record League Sequences:
Successive wins: 8, 1979-80.

Successive draws: 5, 1973-74; 1975-76.

Successive defeats: 7, 1965-66.

Successive matches without defeat: 23, 1987-88.

Successive matches without a win: 16, 1978-79.

Successive matches without conceding a goal: 6, 1980-81.

Successive matches without scoring a goal: 4, 1895-96; 1908-09; 1926-27; 1946-47; 1950-51; 1968-69; 1971-72; 1973-74; 1977-78; 1980-81; 1985-86; 1992-93.

Successive matches without defeat from the start of a season:
10, 1913-14; 1989-90.

Successive matches without a win from the start of a season:
11, 1996-97.

The Numbers Game

Football League/FA Premier League Record and Leading Goalscorers

SEASON	DIVISION	PLAYED	WON	DRAWN	LOST	GOALS FOR	GOALS AGAINST	TOTAL POINTS	POSITION	GOALS SCORED	SCORER
1888-89	FL	22	10	6	6	66	45	26	4th	17	John Southworth
1889-90	FL	22	12	3	7	78	41	27	3rd	22	John Southworth
1890-91	FL	22	11	2	9	52	43	24	6th	26	John Southworth
1891-92	FL	26	10	6	10	58	65	26	9th	22	John Southworth
1892-93	1	30	8	13	9	47	56	29	9th	11	Bill Sawers
1893-94	1	30	16	2	12	69	53	34	4th	14	Harry Chippendale
1894-95	1	30	11	10	9	59	49	32	5th	12	Harry Chippendale
1895-96	1	30	12	5	13	40	50	29	8th	7	Harry Chippendale, James Haydock, Peter Turnbull
1896-97	1	30	11	3	16	35	62	25	14th	7	John Wilkie
1897-98	1	30	7	10	13	39	54	24	15th	9	John Proudfoot
1898-99	1	34	14	8	12	60	52	36	6th	14	Daniel Hurst
1899-00	1	34	13	4	17	49	61	30	14th	11	Arnold Whittaker
1900-01	1	34	12	9	13	39	47	33	9th	8	Arnold Whittaker
1901-02	1	34	15	6	13	52	48	36	4th	16	John Dewhurst
1902-03	1	34	12	5	17	44	63	29	16th	10	Arnold Whittaker
1903-04	1	34	11	6	17	48	60	28	15th	14	Lionel Watson
1904-05	1	34	11	5	18	40	51	27	13th	12	Adam Bowman
1905-06	1	38	16	8	14	54	52	40	9th	15	Adam Bowman
1906-07	1	38	14	7	17	56	59	35	12th	17	Jack Martin
1907-08	1	38	12	12	14	51	63	36	14th=	11	William Davies
1908-09	1	38	14	13	11	61	50	41	4th	19	William Davies
1909-10	1	38	18	9	11	73	55	45	3rd	12	Wattie Aitkenhead
1910-11	1	38	13	11	14	62	54	37	12th	17	William Davies
1911-12	1	38	20	9	9	60	43	49	1st	15	Wattie Aitkenhead
1912-13	1	38	16	13	9	79	43	45	5th	14	Eddie Latheron
1913-14	1	38	20	11	7	78	42	51	1st	28	Danny Shea
1914-15	1	38	18	7	13	83	61	43	3rd	20	Percy Dawson
1919-20	1	42	13	11	18	64	77	37	20th	17	Ernie Hawksworth
1920-21	1	42	13	15	14	57	59	41	11th	17	Percy Dawson
1921-22	1	42	13	12	17	54	57	38	15th	12	Percy Dawson
1922-23	1	42	14	12	16	47	62	40	14th	12	Jock McKay
1923-24	1	42	17	11	14	54	50	45	8th	18	Ted Harper

SEASON	DIVISION	PLAYED	WON	DRAWN	LOST	GOALS FOR	GOALS AGAINST	TOTAL POINTS	POSITION	GOALS SCORED	SCORER
1924-25	1	42	11	13	18	53	66	35	16th	12	John McIntyre, Jock McKay
1925-26	1	42	15	11	16	91	80	41	12th	43	Ted Harper
1926-27	1	42	15	8	19	77	96	38	18th	35	Ted Harper
1927-28	1	42	16	9	17	66	78	41	12th	15	Tom Mitchell
1928-29	1	42	17	11	14	72	63	45	7th	16	Jack Roscamp
1929-30	1	42	19	7	16	99	93	45	6th	21	Clarrie Bourton
1930-31	1	42	17	8	17	83	84	42	10th	19	Jack Bruton
1931-32	1	42	16	6	20	89	95	38	16th	21	Ernie Thompson
1932-33	1	42	14	10	18	76	102	38	15th	17	Ernie Thompson
1933-34	1	42	18	7	17	74	81	43	8th	15	Jack Bruton, Ted Harper
1934-35	1	42	14	11	17	66	78	39	15th	18	Jack Bruton, Ernie Thompson
1935-36	1	42	12	9	21	55	96	33	22nd	15	Ernie Thompson
1936-37	2	42	16	10	16	70	62	42	12th	16	Jack Bruton
1937-38	2	42	14	10	18	71	80	38	16th	20	Len Butt
1938-39	2	42	25	5	12	94	60	55	1st	21	Albert Clarke
1946-47	1	42	14	8	20	45	53	36	17th	12	Jack Smith
1947-48	1	42	11	10	21	54	72	32	21st	15	Les Graham
1948-49	2	42	15	8	19	53	63	38	14th	21	Dennis Westcott
1949-50	2	42	14	10	18	55	60	38	16th	16	Dennis Westcott
1950-51	2	42	19	8	15	65	66	46	6th	13	Les Graham
1951-52	2	42	17	6	19	54	63	40	14th	11	Eddie Quigley
1952-53	2	42	18	8	16	68	65	44	9th	18	Eddie Quigley
1953-54	2	42	23	9	10	86	50	55	3rd	32	Tommy Briggs
1954-55	2	42	22	6	14	114	79	50	6th	33	Tommy Briggs
1955-56	2	42	21	6	15	84	65	48	4th	31	Tommy Briggs
1956-57	2	42	21	10	11	83	75	52	4th	32	Tommy Briggs
1957-58	2	42	22	12	8	93	57	56	2nd	20	Peter Dobing
1958-59	1	42	17	10	15	76	70	44	10th	24	Peter Dobing
1959-60	1	42	16	5	21	60	70	37	17th	18	Peter Dobing
1960-61	1	42	15	13	14	77	76	43	8th	18	Peter Dobing
1961-62	1	42	14	11	17	50	58	39	16th	14	Ian Lawther
1962-63	1	42	15	12	15	79	71	42	11th	23	Fred Pickering
1963-64	1	42	18	10	14	89	65	46	7th	32	Andy McEvoy
1964-65	1	42	16	10	16	83	79	42	10th	29	Andy McEvoy
1965-66	1	42	8	4	30	57	88	20	22nd	10	George Jones, Andy McEvoy
1966-67	2	42	19	13	10	56	46	51	4th	11	John Connelly
1967-68	2	42	16	11	15	56	49	43	8th	8	Mike Ferguson
1968-69	2	42	13	11	18	52	63	37	19th	10	John Connelly, Malcolm Darling, Don Martin

To be part of our success
ring
01254 292929
for more information and full details of all our full-time and part-time courses
or visit us at www.blackburn.ac.uk
Blackburn College exists to serve the educational and cultural needs of the local community
"Outstanding..."
Further Education Funding Council Inspection Report 1999
BLACKBURN COLLEGE

DANNY GREEN HAULAGE
Unit E1, Riverside Ind.Est, Hermitage Street, Rishton, Blackburn, BB1 4NF
DANNY GREEN HAULAGE
Tel: 01254 887176 Fax: 01254 883638

CARL MALLINSON COMMERCIALS
MILLGAP GARAGE, BOLTON ROAD, DARWEN, LANCS, BB3 1DF
COMMERCIAL VEHICLE DEALERS
TEL: 01254 707707

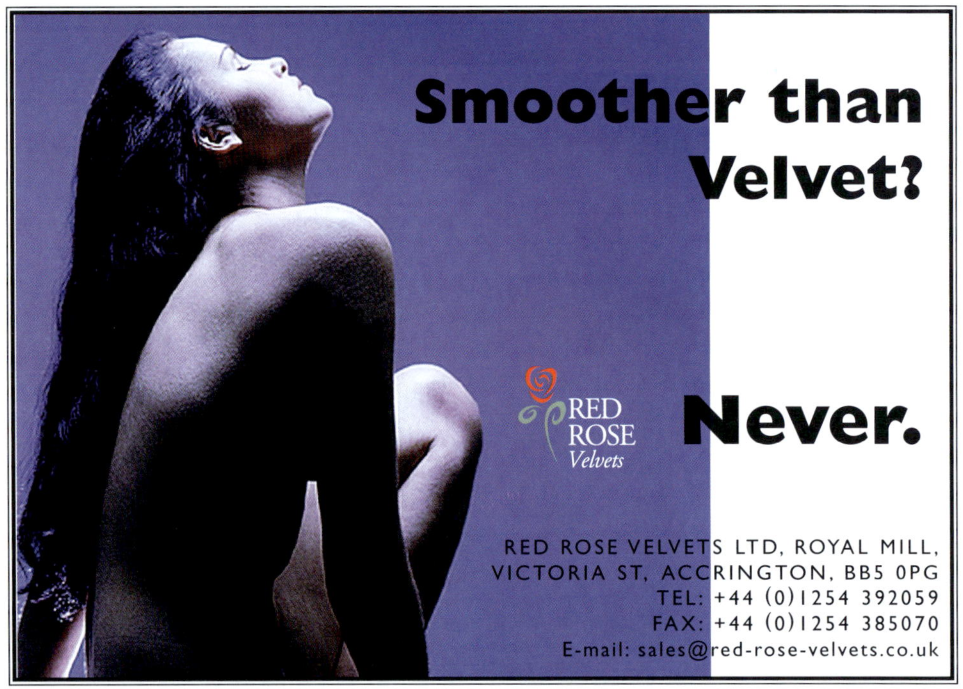
Smoother than Velvet?
RED ROSE Velvets
Never.
RED ROSE VELVETS LTD, ROYAL MILL,
VICTORIA ST, ACCRINGTON, BB5 0PG
TEL: +44 (0)1254 392059
FAX: +44 (0)1254 385070
E-mail: sales@red-rose-velvets.co.uk

SEASON	DIVISION	PLAYED	WON	DRAWN	LOSE	GOALS FOR	GOALS AGAINST	TOTAL POINTS	POSITION	GOALS SCORED	SCORER
1969-70	2	42	20	7	15	54	50	47	8th	13	Don Martin
1970-71	2	42	6	15	21	37	69	27	21st	6	Bryan Conlon, Eamonn Rogers
1971-72	3	46	19	9	18	54	57	47	10th	17	Tony Field
1972-73	3	46	20	15	11	57	47	55	3rd	17	Tony Field
1973-74	3	46	18	10	18	62	64	46	13th	11	Tony Field
1974-75	3	46	22	16	8	68	45	60	1st	15	Don Martin
1975-76	2	42	12	14	16	45	50	38	15th	7	Ken Beamish, Tony Parkes
1976-77	2	42	15	9	18	42	54	39	12th	10	Bobby Svarc
1977-78	2	42	16	13	13	56	60	45	5th	11	Noel Brotherston
1978-79	2	42	10	10	22	41	72	30	22nd	8	Simon Garner
1979-80	3	46	25	9	12	58	36	59	2nd	18	Andy Crawford
1980-81	2	42	16	18	8	42	29	50	4th	10	Kevin Stonehouse
1981-82	2	42	16	11	15	47	43	59	10th	14	Simon Garner
1982-83	2	42	15	12	15	58	58	57	11th	22	Simon Garner
1983-84	2	42	17	16	9	57	46	67	6th	19	Simon Garner
1984-85	2	42	21	10	11	66	41	73	5th	15	Chris Thompson
1985-86	2	42	12	13	17	53	62	49	19th	12	Simon Garner
1986-87	2	42	15	10	17	45	55	55	12th	11	Simon Barker
1987-88	2	44	21	14	9	68	52	77	5th	14	Simon Garner
1988-89	2	46	22	11	13	74	59	77	5th	20	Simon Garner
1989-90	2	46	19	17	10	74	59	74	5th	18	Simon Garner
1990-91	2	46	14	10	22	51	66	52	19th	10	Frank Stapleton
1991-92	2	46	21	11	14	70	53	74	6th	23	David Speedie
1992-93	PL	42	20	11	11	68	46	71	4th	16	Alan Shearer
1993-94	PL	42	25	9	8	63	36	84	2nd	31	Alan Shearer
1994-95	PL	42	27	8	7	80	39	89	1st	34	Alan Shearer
1995-96	PL	38	18	7	13	61	47	61	7th	31	Alan Shearer
1996-97	PL	38	9	15	14	42	43	42	13th	11	Chris Sutton
1997-98	PL	38	16	10	12	57	52	58	6th	18	Chris Sutton
1998-99	PL	38	7	14	17	38	52	35	19th	5	Kevin Gallacher, Ashley Ward

Cup Record

FA Cup - Winners: 1884, 1885, 1886, 1890, 1891, 1928. Finalists: 1882, 1960.

Semi-finalists: 1889, 1893, 1894, 1911, 1912, 1925, 1952, 1958.

Football League Cup - Semi-finalists: 1962, 1993.

Full Members' Cup - Winners: 1987

FA Charity Shield - Winners: 1912.

The Numbers Game

125 Years of Appearances and Goals, 1875-1999

Listed below is every player who has played for Blackburn Rovers Football Club in League & Cup Matches (up to 31.12.99)

	APPEARANCES								GOALS							
	LEAGUE	FOOTBALL LEAGUE PLAY-OFFS/ TEST MATCHES	FA CUP	FOOTBALL LEAGUE CUP	FULL MEMBERS' CUP	FA CHARITY SHIELD	EUROPEAN CHAMPIONS LEAGUE, UEFA CUP	TOTAL	LEAGUE	FOOTBALL LEAGUE PLAY-OFFS/ TEST MATCHES	FA CUP	FOOTBALL LEAGUE CUP	FULL MEMBERS' CUP	FA CHARITY SHIELD	EUROPEAN CHAMPIONS LEAGUE, UEFA CUP	TOTAL
Agnew, SM	2	-	-	2	-	-	-	4	-	-	-	-	-	-	-	-
Ainscow, A	42+23	1+2	-	2+1	4+2	-	-	49+28	5	-	-	1	1	-	-	7
Airey, J	3	-	-	-	-	-	-	3	1	-	-	-	-	-	-	1
Aitken, FM	8	-	-	-	-	-	-	8	1	-	-	-	-	-	-	1
Aitkenhead, WAC	210	-	28	-	-	1	-	239	75	-	18	-	-	2	-	95
Alcock, T	3	-	2	-	-	-	-	5	1	-	-	-	-	-	-	1
Almond, W	58	-	9	-	-	-	-	67	3	-	1	-	-	-	-	4
Anderson, BC	21+7	-	-	-	-	-	-	21+7	7	-	-	-	-	-	-	7
Anderson, CS	13	-	-	-	-	-	-	13	1	-	-	-	-	-	-	1
Anderson, GE	178	4	18	-	-	-	-	200	19	1	-	-	-	-	-	20
Andersson, AP	1+3	-	+1	3	-	-	-	4+4	-	-	-	1	-	-	-	1
Andersson, PJ	7+5	-	1	2	-	-	-	10+5	-	-	-	1	-	-	-	1
Anthony, W	149	-	14	-	-	1	-	164	11	-	3	-	-	-	-	14
Appleby, JP	2	-	-	-	-	-	-	2	-	-	-	-	-	-	-	-
Archibald, S	20	1	1	-	-	-	-	22	6	-	-	-	-	-	-	6
Ardiles, OC	5	1+1	-	-	-	-	-	6+1	-	-	-	-	-	-	-	-
Arentoft, P	94	-	10	4	-	-	-	108	3	-	-	-	-	-	-	3
Arnold, JA	58	-	7	3	-	-	-	68	-	-	-	-	-	-	-	-
Arnott, KW	28+1	-	2	-	-	-	-	30+1	3	-	-	-	-	-	-	3
Arthur, JWH	40	-	35	-	-	-	-	75	-	-	-	-	-	-	-	-
Ashcroft, J	114	-	15	-	-	-	-	129	-	-	-	-	-	-	-	-
Astill, LV	3	-	1	-	-	-	-	4	1	-	-	-	-	-	-	1
Aston, J	12+3	-	-	1	-	-	-	13+3	2	-	-	-	-	-	-	2
Atherton, DL	9+1	-	-	1	-	-	-	10+1	-	-	-	-	-	-	-	-
Atkins, MN	224+33	9	11+3	20+4	5	1+1	2+1	272+42	34	-	-	4	1	-	-	39
Avery, G	-	-	20	-	-	-	-	20	-	-	10	-	-	-	-	10
Baah, PH	1	-	-	-	-	-	-	1	-	-	-	-	-	-	-	-
Bailey, JA	115+5	-	7	7	-	-	-	129+5	1	-	-	-	-	-	-	1
Baldwin, JJ	88	-	8	-	-	-	-	96	-	-	1	-	-	-	-	1
Ball, WH	20	-	-	-	-	-	-	20	-	-	-	-	-	-	-	-
Barker, S	180+2	2	11	9	6	-	-	208+2	35	-	-	4	2	-	-	41
Barron, J	76	-	7	-	-	-	-	83	-	-	-	-	-	-	-	-
Barton, A	-	-	3	-	-	-	-	3	-	-	6	-	-	-	-	6
Barton, D	8	-	-	-	-	-	-	8	1	-	-	-	-	-	-	1
Barton, J	40	-	12	-	-	-	-	52	2	-	2	-	-	-	-	4
Barton, JB	68	-	1	3	-	-	-	72	-	-	-	-	-	-	-	-
Barton, JW	1	-	1	-	-	-	-	2	-	-	-	-	-	-	-	-
Bateson, E	2	-	-	-	-	-	-	2	-	-	-	-	-	-	-	-
Batty, D	53+1	-	5	6	-	1	5	70+1	1	-	-	-	-	-	-	1
Baxendale, F	12	-	1	-	-	-	-	13	3	-	-	-	-	-	-	3

	APPEARANCES								GOALS							
	LEAGUE	FOOTBALL LEAGUE PLAY-OFFS/ TEST MATCHES	FA CUP	FOOTBALL LEAGUE CUP	FULL MEMBERS' CUP	FA CHARITY SHIELD	EUROPEAN CHAMPIONS LEAGUE, UEFA CUP	TOTAL	LEAGUE	FOOTBALL LEAGUE PLAY-OFFS/ TEST MATCHES	FA CUP	FOOTBALL LEAGUE CUP	FULL MEMBERS' CUP	FA CHARITY SHIELD	EUROPEAN CHAMPIONS LEAGUE, UEFA CUP	TOTAL
Baxter, TT	36	-	3	-	-	1	-	40	-	-	-	-	-	-	-	-
Beamish, KG	86	-	3	9	-	-	-	98	18	-	2	5	-	-	-	25
Bean, A	2	-	-	-	-	-	-	2	-	-	-	-	-	-	-	-
Beardall, JT	4+2	-	-	-	-	-	-	4+2	1	-	-	-	-	-	-	1
Beardsmore, RP	1+1	-	-	-	-	-	-	1+1	-	-	-	-	-	-	-	-
Beattie, JM	76	-	5	-	-	-	-	81	17	-	1	-	-	-	-	18
Beattie, JS	1+3	-	+1	2	-	-	-	3+4	-	-	-	-	-	-	-	-
Beckford, JN	3+1	-	-	-	-	-	-	3+1	-	-	-	-	-	-	-	-
Bee, FE	4	-	-	-	-	-	-	4	-	-	-	-	-	-	-	-
Beglin, JM	6	-	-	-	-	-	-	6	-	-	-	-	-	-	-	-
Bell, A	11	-	1	-	-	-	-	12	-	-	-	-	-	-	-	-
Bell, JE	323	-	10	-	-	-	-	333	9	-	-	-	-	-	-	9
Bell, N	57+4	-	2	2	-	-	-	61+4	10	-	-	-	-	-	-	10
Bell, RC	2	-	-	-	-	-	-	2	-	-	-	-	-	-	-	-
Bennett, JW	1	-	-	-	-	-	-	1	-	-	-	-	-	-	-	-
Benson, JR	2	-	-	-	-	-	-	2	1	-	-	-	-	-	-	1
Beresford, J	12	-	2	-	-	-	-	14	4	-	-	-	-	-	-	4
Berg, H	154+5	-	10	16	-	1	8	189+5	4	-	-	-	-	-	-	4
Beverley, J	8	-	14	-	-	-	-	22	-	-	-	-	-	-	-	-
Bibby, J	8	-	-	-	-	-	-	8	-	-	-	-	-	-	-	-
Bimpson, JL	22	-	7	-	-	-	-	29	5	-	3	-	-	-	-	8
Binns, CH	183	-	13	-	-	-	-	196	-	-	-	-	-	-	-	-
Binns, E	23	-	-	-	-	-	-	23	-	-	-	-	-	-	-	-
Birchall, J	39	-	1	-	-	-	-	40	3	-	-	-	-	-	-	3
Birchenall, AJ	17+1	-	2	-	-	-	-	19+1	-	-	-	-	-	-	-	-
Birtwistle, A	-	-	5	-	-	-	-	5	-	-	1	-	-	-	-	1
Birtwistle, R	-	-	4	-	-	-	-	4	-	-	1	-	-	-	-	1
Blackburn, A	4	-	-	-	-	-	-	4	-	-	-	-	-	-	-	-
Blackburn, F	192	2	12	-	-	-	-	206	25	1	5	-	-	-	-	31
Blacklaw, AS	96	-	5	9	-	-	-	110	-	-	-	-	-	-	-	-
Blackshaw, J	2	-	-	-	-	-	-	2	-	-	-	-	-	-	-	-
Blake, NA	17+9	-	3+2	2	-	-	-	22+11	5	-	1	-	-	-	-	6
Blenkhorn, E	-	-	3	-	-	-	-	3	-	-	-	-	-	-	-	-
Blore, R	11	-	-	-	-	-	-	11	-	-	-	-	-	-	-	-
Bogan, T	1	-	-	-	-	-	-	1	-	-	-	-	-	-	-	-
Bohinen, L	40+18	-	2+1	3+2	-	-	-	45+21	7	-	1	1	-	-	-	9
Bond, R	24	-	2	-	-	-	-	26	2	-	1	-	-	-	-	3
Booth, TE	111	3	9	-	-	-	-	123	10	-	1	-	-	-	-	11
Boothman, J	2	-	-	-	-	-	-	2	-	-	-	-	-	-	-	-
Bourton, CFT	63	-	9	-	-	-	-	72	37	-	5	-	-	-	-	42
Bow, W	20	-	3	-	-	-	-	23	2	-	-	-	-	-	-	2
Bowdler, JCH	22	-	4	-	-	-	-	26	5	-	2	-	-	-	-	7
Bowman, A	99	-	5	-	-	-	-	104	42	-	1	-	-	-	-	43
Bracegirdle, E	60	-	5	-	-	-	-	65	6	-	1	-	-	-	-	7
Bradbury, JJL	2	-	-	-	-	-	-	2	-	-	-	-	-	-	-	-
Bradford, DW	58+6	-	5	4	-	-	-	67+6	3	-	-	-	-	-	-	3
Bradshaw, A	11	-	-	-	-	-	-	11	2	-	-	-	-	-	-	2
Bradshaw, PW	78	-	4	5	-	-	-	87	-	-	-	-	-	-	-	-
Bradshaw, W	386	-	39	-	-	1	-	426	36	-	3	-	-	-	-	39
Branagan, JPS	290+4	-	20	18	5	-	-	333+4	5	-	-	-	-	-	-	5

	APPEARANCES								GOALS							
	LEAGUE	FOOTBALL LEAGUE PLAY-OFFS/ TEST MATCHES	FA CUP	FOOTBALL LEAGUE CUP	FULL MEMBERS' CUP	FA CHARITY SHIELD	EUROPEAN CHAMPIONS LEAGUE, UEFA CUP	TOTAL	LEAGUE	FOOTBALL LEAGUE PLAY-OFFS/ TEST MATCHES	FA CUP	FOOTBALL LEAGUE CUP	FULL MEMBERS' CUP	FA CHARITY SHIELD	EUROPEAN CHAMPIONS LEAGUE, UEFA CUP	TOTAL
Brandon, T	216	3	26	-	-	-	-	245	2	-	-	-	-	-	-	2
Bray, J	153	-	19	12	-	-	-	184	2	-	-	-	-	-	-	2
Brayshaw, W	9	-	-	-	-	-	-	9	1	-	-	-	-	-	-	1
Brennan, TJ	13	-	-	-	-	-	-	13	1	-	-	-	-	-	-	1
Briercliffe, T	56	1	4	-	-	-	-	61	11	1	-	-	-	-	-	12
Briggs, TH	194	-	10	-	-	-	-	204	140	-	3	-	-	-	-	143
Britt, MC	8	-	-	1	-	-	-	9	-	-	-	-	-	-	-	-
Britton, F	45	-	3	-	-	-	-	48	8	-	1	-	-	-	-	9
Brooks, EW	3	-	-	-	-	-	-	3	-	-	-	-	-	-	-	-
Broomes, MC	13+7	-	4	1	-	-	-	18+7	1	-	-	-	-	-	-	1
Brotherston, N	307+10	-	24+1	22	2+1	-	-	355+12	40	-	4	2	1	-	-	47
Brown, C	1	-	-	-	-	-	-	1	-	-	-	-	-	-	-	-
Brown, J	4	-	32	-	-	-	-	36	-	-	29	-	-	-	-	29
Brown, RA	26+2	-	2	1+1	1	-	-	30+3	-	-	-	-	-	-	-	-
Bruton, J	324	-	20	-	-	-	-	344	108	-	7	-	-	-	-	115
Bruton, LHR	38	-	4	-	-	-	-	42	23	-	5	-	-	-	-	28
Bryant, CSA	4	-	1	-	-	-	-	5	-	-	-	-	-	-	-	-
Bryant, W	25	-	-	-	-	-	-	25	8	-	-	-	-	-	-	8
Burgin, A	45	-	3	2	-	-	-	50	1	-	-	-	-	-	-	1
Burke, M	34+5	-	1	3	-	-	-	38+5	7	-	1	-	-	-	-	8
Burton, JH	4	-	-	-	-	-	-	4	-	-	-	-	-	-	-	-
Busby, VD	8	-	-	-	-	-	-	8	1	-	-	-	-	-	-	1
Butcher, JM	104	-	5	7	-	-	-	116	-	-	-	-	-	-	-	-
Butt, L	110	-	7	-	-	-	-	117	44	-	4	-	-	-	-	48
Byers, JE	27	-	1	-	-	-	-	28	2	-	-	-	-	-	-	2
Byrne, DS	4	-	-	-	-	-	-	4	-	-	-	-	-	-	-	-
Byrom, J	121+3	-	16	9	-	-	-	146+3	50	-	12	2	-	-	-	64
Byrom, T	13	-	-	-	-	-	-	13	3	-	-	-	-	-	-	3
Cairns, R	26	-	-	-	-	-	-	26	7	-	-	-	-	-	-	7
Calladine, CF	48	-	1	-	-	-	-	49	6	-	1	-	-	-	-	7
Calloway, LJ	17+8	-	2	1+1	-	-	-	20+9	1	-	-	-	-	-	-	1
Calvey, M	6	-	5	-	-	-	-	11	3	-	2	-	-	-	-	5
Cameron, J	64	-	3	-	-	-	-	67	-	-	-	-	-	-	-	-
Cameron, WS	70	-	12	-	-	-	-	82	18	-	1	-	-	-	-	19
Campbell, AF	161	-	23	-	-	-	-	184	7	-	2	-	-	-	-	9
Campbell, H	98	-	15	-	-	-	-	113	22	-	4	-	-	-	-	26
Campbell, J	55	2	1	-	-	-	-	58	10	-	-	-	-	-	-	10
Campbell, JJ	224	-	21	-	-	-	-	245	19	-	1	-	-	-	-	20
Campbell, WC	1	-	-	-	-	-	-	1	-	-	-	-	-	-	-	-
Carsley, LK	31+1	-	2	-	-	-	-	33+1	8	-	1	-	-	-	-	9
Carter, DF	2	-	-	-	-	-	-	2	-	-	-	-	-	-	-	-
Carter, J	43	4	2	-	-	-	-	49	-	-	-	-	-	-	-	-
Carver, J	143	-	3	-	-	-	-	146	2	-	-	-	-	-	-	2
Chadwick, EW	-	-	4	-	-	-	-	4	-	-	3	-	-	-	-	3
Chadwick, FR	11	-	-	-	-	-	-	11	1	-	-	-	-	-	-	1
Chadwick, M	51	-	1	-	-	-	-	52	7	-	-	-	-	-	-	7
Chambers, P	33	-	-	-	-	-	-	33	-	-	-	-	-	-	-	-
Chapman, GR	138	-	14	-	-	-	-	152	34	-	8	-	-	-	-	42
Chappell, LA	7	-	-	-	-	-	-	7	-	-	-	-	-	-	-	-

	APPEARANCES								GOALS							
	LEAGUE	FOOTBALL LEAGUE PLAY-OFFS/ TEST MATCHES	FA CUP	FOOTBALL LEAGUE CUP	FULL MEMBERS' CUP	FA CHARITY SHIELD	EUROPEAN CHAMPIONS LEAGUE, UEFA CUP	TOTAL	LEAGUE	FOOTBALL LEAGUE PLAY-OFFS/ TEST MATCHES	FA CUP	FOOTBALL LEAGUE CUP	FULL MEMBERS' CUP	FA CHARITY SHIELD	EUROPEAN CHAMPIONS LEAGUE, UEFA CUP	TOTAL
Charter, R	13+5	-	+1	-	-	-	-	13+6	-	-	-	-	-	-	-	-
Chippendale, H	134	-	13	-	-	-	-	147	50	-	2	-	-	-	-	52
Chivers, FC	48	-	7	-	-	-	-	55	2	-	1	-	-	-	-	3
Christie, NT	43	-	7	-	-	-	-	50	2	-	1	-	-	-	-	3
Clark, SJH	1	-	-	-	-	-	-	1	-	-	-	-	-	-	-	-
Clarke, A	38	-	4	-	-	-	-	42	21	-	2	-	-	-	-	23
Clayton, K	72	-	5	-	-	-	-	77	-	-	-	-	-	-	-	-
Clayton, R	579+2	-	56	28	-	-	-	663+2	15	-	1	-	-	-	-	16
Cleghorn, T	45	-	3	-	-	-	-	48	3	-	-	-	-	-	-	3
Clennell, J	26	-	1	-	-	1	-	28	12	-	-	-	-	-	-	12
Clinton, TJ	6	-	2	-	-	-	-	8	-	-	-	-	-	-	-	-
Clough, AE	1	-	-	-	-	-	-	1	-	-	-	-	-	-	-	-
Cockshutt, JW	1	-	-	-	-	-	-	1	-	-	-	-	-	-	-	-
Coddington, JW	72+1	-	5	6	-	-	-	83+1	3	-	-	-	-	-	-	3
Coleman, C	27+1	-	2	2	-	-	-	31+1	-	-	-	-	-	-	-	-
Collier, DJ	27	-	-	3	1	-	-	31	-	-	-	-	-	-	-	-
Comstive, PT	3+3	-	-	-	-	-	-	3+3	-	-	-	-	-	-	-	-
Conlon, B	43+2	-	2	3+1	-	-	-	48+3	7	-	-	-	-	-	-	7
Connelly, JM	148+1	-	6	9	-	-	-	163+1	36	-	2	1	-	-	-	39
Cook, L	76	-	8	-	-	-	-	84	-	-	-	-	-	-	-	-
Coombs, EH	6	-	-	-	-	-	-	6	-	-	-	-	-	-	-	-
Cope, H	25	-	-	-	-	-	-	25	-	-	-	-	-	-	-	-
Coughlin, R	22+2	-	-	1+1	-	-	-	23+3	-	-	-	-	-	-	-	-
Coupe, T	1	-	-	-	-	-	-	1	-	-	-	-	-	-	-	-
Cowans, GS	49+1	3	5	4	-	-	-	61+1	2	-	1	-	-	-	-	3
Cowell, A	279	-	26	-	-	1	-	306	-	-	-	-	-	-	-	-
Coxon, EG	10	-	-	-	-	-	-	10	-	-	-	-	-	-	-	-
Crabtree, JJ	12	-	-	-	-	-	-	12	-	-	-	-	-	-	-	-
Craig, J	44+4	-	3	3+1	-	-	-	50+5	8	-	1	1	-	-	-	10
Craig, RM	8	-	-	2	-	-	-	10	3	-	-	-	-	-	-	3
Crawford, A	56	-	8	4	-	-	-	68	21	-	5	-	-	-	-	26
Crawford, JC	155	-	17	-	-	1	-	173	-	-	-	-	-	-	-	-
Crawford, R	5	-	-	-	-	-	-	5	-	-	-	-	-	-	-	-
Crawley, FP	24	-	2	-	-	-	-	26	1	-	-	-	-	-	-	1
Crisp, J	98	-	10	-	-	-	-	108	18	-	1	-	-	-	-	19
Croft, G	33+7	-	4+2	6	-	-	-	43+9	1	-	-	-	-	-	-	1
Crompton, A	2+2	-	-	-	-	-	-	2+2	-	-	-	-	-	-	-	-
Crompton, GE	35	-	1	-	-	-	-	36	20	-	-	-	-	-	-	20
Crompton, R	529	-	46	-	-	1	-	576	14	-	-	-	-	-	-	14
Crompton, W	20	-	-	-	-	-	-	20	5	-	-	-	-	-	-	5
Crook, JA	9	-	-	-	-	-	-	9	2	-	-	-	-	-	-	2
Crook, W	218	-	19	-	-	-	-	237	2	-	-	-	-	-	-	2
Crossan, E	287	-	15	-	-	-	-	302	73	-	1	-	-	-	-	74
Crowe, C	51	-	5	6	-	-	-	62	6	-	1	4	-	-	-	11
Cunliffe, A	129	-	11	-	-	-	-	140	47	-	8	-	-	-	-	55
Cunliffe, T	1	-	-	-	-	-	-	1	-	-	-	-	-	-	-	-
Curry, SP	25+13	+2	+1	3+2	2+1	-	-	30+19	6	-	-	-	1	-	-	7
Curtis, J	9+1	-	-	2	-	-	-	11+1	-	-	-	-	-	-	-	-

	APPEARANCES								GOALS							
	LEAGUE	FOOTBALL LEAGUE PLAY-OFFS/ TEST MATCHES	FA CUP	FOOTBALL LEAGUE CUP	FULL MEMBERS' CUP	FA CHARITY SHIELD	EUROPEAN CHAMPIONS LEAGUE, UEFA CUP	TOTAL	LEAGUE	FOOTBALL LEAGUE PLAY-OFFS/ TEST MATCHES	FA CUP	FOOTBALL LEAGUE CUP	FULL MEMBERS' CUP	FA CHARITY SHIELD	EUROPEAN CHAMPIONS LEAGUE, UEFA CUP	TOTAL
Dahlin, M	13+13	-	+1	2	-	-	+1	15+15	4	-	-	2	-	-	-	6
Dailly, CE	36+3		2	3	-	-	2	43+3	2	_-	-	-	-	-	-	2
Daly, PJ	3	-	-	1	-	-	-	4	-	-	-	-	-	-	-	-
Darling, M	114+14	-	8	4+1	-	-	-	126+15	30	-	4	-	-	-	-	34
Darroch, J	17	-	1	-	-	-	-	18	-	-	-	-	-	-	-	-
Davidson, CI	48+1	-	4	3+1	-	-	1+1	56+3	1	-	-	-	-	-	-	1
Davies, KC	11+12	-	2	3	-	-	1	17+12	1	-	1	-	-	-	-	2
Davies, W	132	-	11	-	-	-	-	143	67	-	3	-	-	-	-	70
Davis, E	24	-	1	-	-	-	-	25	-	-	-	-	-	-	-	-
Dawson, A	18	-	-	-	-	-	-	18	4	-	-	-	-	-	-	4
Dawson, AJ	32+8	1+1	1	3	1+1	-	-	38+10	-	-	-	-	-	-	-	-
Dawson, PH	140	-	11	-	-	-	-	151	71	-	2	-	-	-	-	73
Dennis, W	5	-	-	-	-	-	-	5	-	-	-	-	-	-	-	-
Dennison, H	3	-	-	-	-	-	-	3	-	-	-	-	-	-	-	-
Derbyshire, JE	11	-	-	-	-	-	-	11	-	-	-	-	-	-	-	-
Devine, P	8	-	-	-	-	-	-	8	2	-	-	-	-	-	-	2
Devlin, H	1	-	-	-	-	-	-	1	-	-	-	-	-	-	-	-
DeVries, RS	13	-	1	3	-	-	-	17	-	-	-	-	-	-	-	-
Dewar, G	174	-	22	-	-	-	-	196	7	-	3	-	-	-	-	10
Dewhurst, J	169	-	13	-	-	-	-	182	43	-	4	-	-	-	-	47
Dewhurst, RM	13	-	-	1	1	-	-	15	-	-	-	-	-	-	-	-
Diamond, AJ	9+17	-	-	-	1+1	-	-	10+18	3	-	-	-	-	-	-	3
Dickie, P	19	-	2	-	-	-	-	21	1	-	-	-	-	-	-	1
Dickins, MJ	1	-	-	-	-	-	-	1	-	-	-	-	-	-	-	-
Dix, RW	38	-	2	-	-	-	-	40	14	-	1	-	-	-	-	15
Dixon, ES	29	-	2	-	-	-	-	31	1	-	2	-	-	-	-	3
Dobing. PA	179	-	22	4	-	-	-	205	88	-	16	-	-	-	-	104
Dobson, AJ	36+5	-	2	5	1	-	-	44+5	-	-	-	-	-	-	-	-
Doig, JE	1	-	-	-	-	-	-	1	-	-	-	-	-	-	-	-
Donis, G	11+11	-	+1	3	-	-	-	14+12	2	-	-	-	-	-	-	2
Donnelly, DC	1+1	-	-	-	-	-	-	1+1	-	-	-	-	-	-	-	-
Donnelly, J	8	-	2	-	-	-	-	10	-	-	-	-	-	-	-	-
Dougan, AD	59	-	14	3	-	-	-	76	26	-	4	4	-	-	-	34
Douglas, B	438	-	39+1	25	-	-	-	502+1	101	-	9	5	-	-	-	115
Douglas, J	34	-	42	-	-	-	-	76	-	-	8	-	-	-	-	8
Downes, SF	6	-	-	-	-	-	-	6	-	-	-	-	-	-	-	-
Duckworth, F	60	-	3	-	-	-	-	63	-	-	-	-	-	-	-	-
Duckworth, J	-	-	13	-	-	-	-	13	-	-	7	-	-	-	-	7
Duckworth, JC	5	-	2	-	-	-	-	7	-	-	-	-	-	-	-	-
Duckworth, TC	1	-	1	-	-	-	-	2	-	-	-	-	-	-	-	-
Duerden, J	2	-	-	-	-	-	-	2	-	-	-	-	-	-	-	-
Duff, DA	49+25	-	7+2	7+1	-	-	1	64+28	6	-	2	1	-	-	-	9
Duncan, WM	2	-	1	-	-	-	-	3	-	-	-	-	-	-	-	-
Dunkley, AE	4	-	-	-	-	-	-	4	1	-	-	-	-	-	-	1
Dunn, DJI	18+6	-	2+1	4+1	-	-	-	24+8	1	-	-	1	-	-	-	2
Dunning, W	10+3	-	-	-	-	-	-	10+3	2	-	-	-	-	-	-	2
Duxbury, M	25+2	-	2	1	+1	-	-	28+3	-	-	-	-	-	-	-	-

	APPEARANCES								GOALS							
	LEAGUE	FOOTBALL LEAGUE PLAY-OFFS/ TEST MATCHES	FA CUP	FOOTBALL LEAGUE CUP	FULL MEMBERS' CUP	FA CHARITY SHIELD	EUROPEAN CHAMPIONS LEAGUE, UEFA CUP	TOTAL	LEAGUE	FOOTBALL LEAGUE PLAY-OFFS/ TEST MATCHES	FA CUP	FOOTBALL LEAGUE CUP	FULL MEMBERS' CUP	FA CHARITY SHIELD	EUROPEAN CHAMPIONS LEAGUE, UEFA CUP	TOTAL
Eastham, JB	48	-	4	-	-	-	-	52	-	-	-	-	-	-	-	-
Eccles, TS	33+13	-	1	2	-	-	-	36+13	6	-	-	1	-	-	-	7
Eckersley, W	406	-	26	-	-	-	-	432	20	-	1	-	-	-	-	21
Eddleston, J	7	-	-	-	-	-	-	7	3	-	-	-	-	-	-	3
Edds, EF	18	-	1	-	-	-	-	19	3	-	1	-	-	-	-	4
Edge, AS	9	-	-	-	-	-	-	9	-	-	-	-	-	-	-	-
Ellis, R	1	-	-	-	-	-	-	1	1	-	-	-	-	-	-	1
Else, F	187	-	18	16	-	-	-	221	-	-	-	-	-	-	-	-
Elvy, R	192	-	16	-	-	-	-	208	-	-	-	-	-	-	-	-
Endean, B	65+14	-	5	3+1	-	-	-	73+15	18	-	-	1	-	-	-	19
England, HM	165	-	12	7	-	-	-	184	21	-	-	-	-	-	-	21
Evans, L	2	-	-	-	-	-	-	2	-	-	-	-	-	-	-	-
Evans, RO	104	-	9	-	-	-	-	113	-	-	-	-	-	-	-	-
Fairbrother, RW	1	-	-	-	-	-	-	1	-	-	-	-	-	-	-	-
Farrell, GW	21+1	-	2	-	-	-	-	23+1	1	-	-	-	-	-	-	1
Faulkner, R	9	-	-	-	-	-	-	9	-	-	-	-	-	-	-	-
Fawcett, WF	5	-	-	-	-	-	-	5	1	-	-	-	-	-	-	1
Fazackerley, DW	593+3	-	40	38	-	-	-	671+3	24	-	1	1	-	-	-	26
Fear, KW	5	-	1	-	-	-	-	6	2	-	-	-	-	-	-	2
Fecitt, HL	21	-	23	-	-	-	-	44	13	-	13	-	-	-	-	26
Fenton, GA	9+18	-	+1	+2	-	-	-	9+21	7	-	-	-	-	-	-	7
Fenton, WH	33	-	1	-	-	-	-	34	7	-	-	-	-	-	-	7
Ferguson, J	32	-	-	-	-	-	-	32	1	-	-	-	-	-	-	1
Ferguson, MK	220	-	15	14	-	-	-	249	29	-	1	6	-	-	-	36
Fettis, AW	9+2	-	1	-	-	-	-	10+2	-	-	-	-	-	-	-	-
Field, A	104+2	-	10	4	-	-	-	118+2	45	-	7	2	-	-	-	54
Filan, JR	47	-	4	3	-	-	-	54	-	-	-	-	-	-	-	-
Finnigan, A	21+15	-	5	3	3+1	-	-	32+16	-	-	1	-	1	-	-	2
Flitcroft, GW	68+6	-	3+1	3+1	-	-	2	76+8	5	-	-	1	-	-	1	7
Flowers, TD	175+2	-	13+1	14	-	2	10	214+3	-	-	-	-	-	-	-	-
Forbes, GP	2	-	1	-	-	-	-	3	1	-	-	-	-	-	-	1
Forbes, J	106	-	20	-	-	-	-	126	1	-	1	-	-	-	-	2
Forrest, JH (Snr)	148	-	47	-	-	-	-	195	2	-	5	-	-	-	-	7
Forrest, JH (Jnr)	16	-	2	-	-	-	-	18	-	-	-	-	-	-	-	-
Fowler, M	36+2	-	1	3	-	-	-	40+2	-	-	-	-	-	-	-	-
France, H	4	-	-	-	-	-	-	4	-	-	-	-	-	-	-	-
Frandsen, P	14+1	-	2	-	-	-	-	16+1	3	-	1	-	-	-	-	4
Fraser, NJ	-	-	1	-	-	-	-	1	-	-	1	-	-	-	-	1
Fryatt, JE	29+8	-	4	-	-	-	-	33+8	5	-	3	-	-	-	-	8
Gale, AP	15	-	-	2	-	1	2	20	-	-	-	-	-	-	-	-
Gallacher, B	4	-	-	-	-	-	-	4	-	-	-	-	-	-	-	-
Gallacher, KW	132+12	-	13	8+2	-	1	+1	154+15	46	-	4	3	-	-	-	53
Gallacher, P	11	-	-	-	-	-	-	11	-	-	-	-	-	-	-	-
Garbett, TG	90	-	9	4	-	-	-	103	6	-	1	-	-	-	-	7
Garbutt, W	81	-	4	-	-	-	-	85	10	-	-	-	-	-	-	10
Garner, S	455+29	7+1	24+5	32+2	10	-	-	528+37	168	2	7	11	4	-	-	192
Garstang, H	3	-	-	-	-	-	-	3	-	-	-	-	-	-	-	-

	APPEARANCES								GOALS							
	LEAGUE	FOOTBALL LEAGUE PLAY-OFFS/ TEST MATCHES	FA CUP	FOOTBALL LEAGUE CUP	FULL MEMBERS' CUP	FA CHARITY SHIELD	EUROPEAN CHAMPIONS LEAGUE, UEFA CUP	TOTAL	LEAGUE	FOOTBALL LEAGUE PLAY-OFFS/ TEST MATCHES	FA CUP	FOOTBALL LEAGUE CUP	FULL MEMBERS' CUP	FA CHARITY SHIELD	EUROPEAN CHAMPIONS LEAGUE, UEFA CUP	TOTAL
Garstang, J	4	-	-	-	-	-	-	4	-	-	-	-	-	-	-	-
Gate, HW	4	-	-	-	-	-	-	4	1	-	-	-	-	-	-	1
Gayle, HA	97+19	8	5+2	6+3	3+1	-	-	119+25	29	3	-	1	1	-	-	34
Gennoe, TW	289	8	18	15	4	-	-	334	-	-	-	-	-	-	-	-
Gibson, TK	-	-	1	-	-	-	-	1	-	-	-	-	-	-	-	-
Gilhespy, TWC	5	-	-	-	-	-	-	5	1	-	-	-	-	-	-	1
Gill, WJ	-	-	-	3	-	-	-	3	-	-	-	-	-	-	-	-
Gillespie, KR	15+6	-	4	2	-	-	-	21+6	1	-	1	-	-	-	-	2
Gillespie, M	6	-	-	-	-	-	-	6	1	-	-	-	-	-	-	1
Gilliver, AH	32+2	-	1	4	-	-	-	37+2	9	-	-	-	-	-	-	9
Given, SJJ	2	-	-	+1	-	-	-	2+1	-	-	-	-	-	-	-	-
Glaister, G	8	-	2	-	-	-	-	10	1	-	-	-	-	-	-	1
Glenn, DA	23+1	-	3	-	-	-	-	26+1	-	-	-	-	-	-	-	-
Glover, A	64	-	7	-	-	-	-	71	4	-	1	-	-	-	-	5
Glover, JW	25	1	1	-	-	-	-	27	-	-	-	-	-	-	-	-
Godwin, V	27	-	-	-	-	-	-	27	6	-	-	-	-	-	-	6
Goodwin, FJ	63+1	-	1	4	-	-	-	68+1	4	-	-	-	-	-	-	4
Gordon, P	12	-	3	-	-	-	-	15	2	-	1	-	-	-	-	3
Gorman J	213	-	12	-	-	-	-	225	-	-	-	-	-	-	-	-
Gormlie, WJ	44	-	-	-	-	-	-	44	-	-	-	-	-	-	-	-
Gow, J	15	-	3	-	-	-	-	18	-	-	-	-	-	-	-	-
Graham, L	150	-	7	-	-	-	-	157	42	-	2	-	-	-	-	44
Gray, D	107	-	4	-	-	-	-	111	5	-	-	-	-	-	-	5
Grayson, SN	17+3	-	1	+1	-	-	-	18+4	-	-	-	-	-	-	-	-
Green, A	-	-	2	-	-	-	-	2	-	-	-	-	-	-	-	-
Greenwood, DH	-	-	10	-	-	-	-	10	-	-	-	-	-	-	-	-
Gregory, DH	5	-	-	1	-	-	-	6	3	-	-	1	-	-	-	4
Grew, MS	13	-	-	1	-	-	-	14	-	-	-	-	-	-	-	-
Griffiths, B	2	-	-	-	-	-	-	2	-	-	-	-	-	-	-	-
Groves, A	65	-	3	-	-	-	-	68	26	-	-	-	-	-	-	26
Gudmundsson, N	1+5	-	-	-	-	-	-	1+5	-	-	-	-	-	-	-	-
Guest, WF	88	-	6	-	-	-	-	94	30	-	2	-	-	-	-	32
Hall, C	79	-	9	-	-	-	-	88	26	-	4	-	-	-	-	30
Hall, FW	29	-	1	-	-	-	-	30	-	-	-	-	-	-	-	-
Hall, G	1	-	-	-	-	-	-	1	1	-	-	-	-	-	-	1
Halsall, WG	63	-	6	-	-	-	-	69	4	-	1	-	-	-	-	5
Hamill, A	21	-	3	-	-	-	-	24	4	-	-	-	-	-	-	4
Hamill, KJ	1	-	-	-	-	-	-	1	-	-	-	-	-	-	-	-
Hamilton, D	104+10	-	1+1	7	-	-	-	112+11	7	-	-	-	-	-	-	7
Hand, J	2	-	-	-	-	-	-	2	-	-	-	-	-	-	-	-
Hannah, G	3	-	-	-	-	-	-	3	-	-	-	-	-	-	-	-
Hardy, A	42	-	-	-	-	-	-	42	-	-	-	-	-	-	-	-
Hardy, GG	7	-	-	-	-	-	-	7	-	-	-	-	-	-	-	-
Hardy, JH	1	-	-	-	-	-	-	1	-	-	-	-	-	-	-	-
Haresnape, R	9	-	4	-	-	-	-	13	2	-	6	-	-	-	-	8
Hargreaves, A	2	-	-	-	-	-	-	2	-	-	-	-	-	-	-	-
Hargreaves, DG	2	-	-	-	-	-	-	2	-	-	-	-	-	-	-	-
Hargreaves, FW	-	-	12	-	-	-	-	12	-	-	1	-	-	-	-	1

Pilkington Bridge Car Sales Ltd
Car Loans Guaranteed
Need A Car But Can't Get Credit?
all Us Today
Over 50 Cars In Stock
Open 7 Days a Week
reephone
0800 1950662
Pilkington Bridge Car Sales
Moorfield Industrial Estate, Burnley Road
Altham, Accrington BB5 5TX
Tel: (01254) 395520 Fax: (01254) 398154
Mobile: 0410 648227

Legal & Property
Financial & Business
Independent Legal & Business Services
Telephone & Fax
01254 692482
Mobile
0410 033489
10 Preston New Road,
Blackburn BB2 1AW

GARETH'S FLORIST
Floral Designers For All Occasions
15% Discount on all items over £20 For Rovers supporters and their families
Free Delivery Service
Order and Pay by Phone
Tel: 01254 885492
49 Queen Street,
Great Harwood

The Hake Boat Chippy
Blackburn Boulvard
Now under New Management
Fresh Fish Daily
New Potatoes
Hollands Pies
Also Try:
Our Famous Homemade Cyprus Curries & Greek Salads
Now also serving All Day Breakfast to eat-in or Take-away Plus Much More!!
For Orders Phone Pete On:
696966

Brooks & Company
Provident Garage
Registered office:
Provident Yard,
Cotton Hall Street, Darwen,
Lancs
Telephone:
01254 702105
VS
Specialists in Accident Insurance Work, Mechanical Repairs and Servicing
M.O.T. Work

neil·howard
vodafone
Specialist in all types of mobile communications
Full range of mobile phones and accessories
Visit our web site
Units 1 and 2
Lower Philips Road
Whitebirk Industrial Estate
Blackburn
Lancashire BBI 5PG
Telephone: 01254 51918
Facsimile: 01254 678602
www.neilhoward.co.uk
vodafone

TOMMY BLANK TYRES
TOYO ONLY THE BEST
Proxes T1S
EXHAUSTS • TYRES • BATTERIES
Established 1963
Best Prices in the North West
✔ Performance Tyre Specialist
✔ All Leading Brands Supplied & Fitted
✔ Computerised Wheel Balancing
✔ Servicing
✔ Batteries
✔ High Spec Remoulds
✔ Wheel Alignment
✔ Puncture Repairs While-U-Wait
✔ Fast Friendly Service
✔ All Work Guaranteed
✔ Open 6 Days Monday - Saturday
MasterCard
SWITCH
VISA
Now Stocking Alloy Wheels
☎ 01254 235406
☎ 01254 398571
T. BLANK TYRES LTD
18 Dale Street, Accrington

Established since 1981
S & J
WELDING
WELDING CONTRACTORS IN STAINLESS STEEL AND MILD STEEL PIPEWORK ALSO GENERAL SITE FABRICATIONS
575 Preston Old Road
Cherry Tree, Blackburn
Lancashire BB2 5NU
Site No: 01772-877444
Fax: 01772-877444
Mobile: 07973-417501

	APPEARANCES								GOALS							
	LEAGUE	FOOTBALL LEAGUE PLAY-OFFS/ TEST MATCHES	FA CUP	FOOTBALL LEAGUE CUP	FULL MEMBERS' CUP	FA CHARITY SHIELD	EUROPEAN CHAMPIONS LEAGUE, UEFA CUP	TOTAL	LEAGUE	FOOTBALL LEAGUE PLAY-OFFS/ TEST MATCHES	FA CUP	FOOTBALL LEAGUE CUP	FULL MEMBERS' CUP	FA CHARITY SHIELD	EUROPEAN CHAMPIONS LEAGUE, UEFA CUP	TOTAL
Hargreaves, John	-	-	11	-	-	-	-	11	-	-	5	-	-	-	-	5
Hargreaves, Joshua	54	2	5	-	-	-	-	61	19	-	-	-	-	-	-	19
Hargreaves, T	4	-	-	-	-	-	-	4	2	-	-	-	-	-	-	2
Harkness, S	8	-	1	1+1	-	-	-	10+1	-	-	-	-	-	-	-	-
Harper, EC	171	-	6	-	-	-	-	177	121	-	1	-	-	-	-	122
Harris, J	35	-	1	-	-	-	-	36	14	-	-	-	-	-	-	14
Harrison, MJ	160	-	14	7	-	-	-	181	40	-	2	1	-	-	-	43
Hartley, D	6	-	-	-	-	-	-	6	-	-	-	-	-	-	-	-
Harvey, A	1	-	-	-	-	-	-	1	-	-	-	-	-	-	-	-
Haverty, J	27	-	-	4	-	-	-	31	1	-	-	-	-	-	-	1
Hawkins, GN	108+1	-	4	8	-	-	-	120+1	4	-	-	-	-	-	-	4
Hawksworth, E	96	-	4	-	-	-	-	100	34	-	-	-	-	-	-	34
Haworth, G	-	-	2	-	-	-	-	2	-	-	-	-	-	-	-	-
Haworth, Robert	122	-	7	-	-	-	-	129	5	-	-	-	-	-	-	5
Haworth, Ronald	25	-	-	-	-	-	-	25	7	-	-	-	-	-	-	7
Haydock, J	66	-	13	-	-	-	-	79	21	-	6	-	-	-	-	27
Hayhurst, S	27	-	-	-	-	-	-	27	-	-	-	-	-	-	-	-
Healless, H	360	-	36	-	-	1	-	397	12	-	1	-	-	-	-	13
Heaton, JM	169+2	-	9	10	-	-	-	188+2	1	-	-	-	-	-	-	1
Heaton, T	57	-	2	-	-	-	-	59	1	-	-	-	-	-	-	1
Helliwell, D	15	-	-	1	-	-	-	16	1	-	-	-	-	-	-	1
Henchoz, S	70	-	6	3+1	-	-	2	81+1	-	-	-	-	-	-	-	-
Hendry, ECJ	328+8	9	20+1	27	7	1	7	399+9	34	-	-	-	1	-	-	35
Herron, A	4	-	-	-	-	-	-	4	-	-	-	-	-	-	-	-
Heyes, J	-	-	12	-	-	-	-	12	-	-	1	-	-	-	-	1
Heywood, J	15	-	1	-	-	-	-	16	-	-	-	-	-	-	-	-
Hickman, MFT	23+3	-	-	2	-	-	-	25+3	8	-	-	-	-	-	-	8
Higgins, G	53	-	3	-	-	-	-	56	-	-	-	-	-	-	-	-
Hildersley, RC	25+5	-	3	+1	3	-	-	31+6	4	-	1	-	-	-	-	5
Hill, B	34+3	-	2	4	-	-	-	40+3	4	-	-	1	-	-	-	5
Hill, KJ	89+7	+2	5+1	6	3	-	-	103+10	4	-	-	1	-	-	-	5
Hilton, PJ	16	-	-	5	-	-	-	21	2	-	-	-	-	-	-	2
Hindle, H	2	-	-	-	-	-	-	2	-	-	-	-	-	-	-	-
Hindson, G	10	-	-	-	-	-	-	10	-	-	-	-	-	-	-	-
Hird, K	129+3	-	8	7+1	-	-	-	144+4	20	-	-	1	-	-	-	21
Hodkinson, J	228	-	16	-	-	-	-	244	19	-	1	-	-	-	-	20
Holden, A	1	-	-	1	-	-	-	2	-	-	-	-	-	-	-	-
Holden, W	1	-	-	-	-	-	-	1	-	-	-	-	-	-	-	-
Hole, BG	79	-	2	7	-	-	-	88	13	-	-	2	-	-	-	15
Holland, PB	116	-	9	-	-	-	-	125	24	-	1	-	-	-	-	25
Holliday, KJ	29	-	1	-	-	-	-	30	-	-	-	-	-	-	-	-
Holmes, MJE	8+1	-	-	-	-	-	2+1	10+2	1	-	-	-	-	-	-	1
Holmes, W	21	-	4	-	-	-	-	25	16	-	3	-	-	-	-	19
Holt, DE	10	-	-	1	-	-	-	11	-	-	-	-	-	-	-	-
Holt, WK	78	-	2	-	-	-	-	80	-	-	-	-	-	-	-	-
Hope, P	6	-	2	-	-	-	-	8	-	-	-	-	-	-	-	-
Hopwood, W	-	-	1	-	-	-	-	1	-	-	-	-	-	-	-	-
Hornby, AN	-	-	1	-	-	-	-	1	-	-	1	-	-	-	-	1
Horne, JK	2	-	3	-	-	-	-	5	-	-	-	-	-	-	-	-

	APPEARANCES								GOALS							
	LEAGUE	FOOTBALL LEAGUE PLAY-OFFS/ TEST MATCHES	FA CUP	FOOTBALL LEAGUE CUP	FULL MEMBERS' CUP	FA CHARITY SHIELD	EUROPEAN CHAMPIONS LEAGUE, UEFA CUP	TOTAL	LEAGUE	FOOTBALL LEAGUE PLAY-OFFS/ TEST MATCHES	FA CUP	FOOTBALL LEAGUE CUP	FULL MEMBERS' CUP	FA CHARITY SHIELD	EUROPEAN CHAMPIONS LEAGUE, UEFA CUP	TOTAL
Horne, WE	7	-	-	-	-	-	-	7	-	-	-	-	-	-	-	-
Horrey, RG	3	-	-	1	-	-	-	4	-	-	-	-	-	-	-	-
Horton, H	92	-	6	-	-	-	-	98	5	-	-	-	-	-	-	5
Hosie, J	3	-	-	-	-	-	-	3	-	-	-	-	-	-	-	-
Hough, WA	49	-	7	-	-	-	-	56	-	-	-	-	-	-	-	-
Houlker, AE	151	3	9	-	-	-	-	163	2	-	-	-	-	-	-	2
Howorth, R	-	-	12	-	-	-	-	12	-	-	-	-	-	-	-	-
Hoy, R	13+6	-	1	+2	-	-	-	14+8	-	-	-	-	-	-	-	-
Hoyne, J	2	-	-	-	-	-	-	2	-	-	-	-	-	-	-	-
Hudson, GA	4	-	-	-	-	-	-	4	1	-	-	-	-	-	-	1
Hughes, JI	47	-	3	-	-	-	-	50	-	-	-	-	-	-	-	-
Hughes, WA	27	-	1	-	-	-	-	28	-	-	-	-	-	-	-	-
Hulme, JHA	73	-	9	-	-	-	-	82	6	-	2	-	-	-	-	8
Hulse, BD	85	3	5	-	-	-	-	93	22	-	3	-	-	-	-	25
Hunter, A	84	-	2	5	-	-	-	91	1	-	-	-	-	-	-	1
Hurst, DJ	53	2	5	-	-	-	-	60	17	2	-	-	-	-	-	19
Hutchins, D	37+3	-	1+1	2+1	-	-		40+5	6	-	-	-	-	-	-	6
Hutt, G	10	-	-	-	-	-	-	10	1	-	-	-	-	-	-	1
Hutton, J	127	-	19	-	-	-	-	146	4	-	1	-	-	-	-	5
Imrie, WN	165	-	11	-	-	-	-	176	23	-	1	-	-	-	-	24
Inglis, J	-	-	3	-	-	-	-	3	-	-	1	-	-	-	-	1
Ireland, SP	+1	-	-	-	-	-	-	+1	-	-	-	-	-	-	-	-
Irvine, JA	40+18	-	-	3	+1	-	-	43+19	3	-	-	-	-	-	-	3
Isherwood, RE	49	-	2	6	-	-	-	57	9	-	-	-	-	-	-	9
Jackson, H	1	-	1	-	-	-	-	2	-	-	-	-	-	-	-	-
Jackson, JT	26	2	1	-	-	-	-	29	10	-	-	-	-	-	-	10
Jacques, TE	2	-	-	-	-	-	-	2	-	-	-	-	-	-	-	-
Jansen, MB	18+5	-	-	1+1	-	-	-	19+6	4	-	-	2	-	-	-	6
Jefferson, T	-	-	1	-	-	-	-	1	-	-	-	-	-	-	-	-
Johnrose, L	20+22	-	+3	2+1	2	-	-	24+26	11	-	-	1	-	-	-	12
Johnson, A	1	-	-	-	-	-	-	1	-	-	-	-	-	-	-	-
Johnson, DM	18+10	-	+2	6+1	-	-	+1	24+14	1	-	-	-	-	-	-	1
Johnston, J	14	-	-	-	-	-	-	14	-	-	-	-	-	-	-	-
Johnston, TB	36	-	2	-	-	-	-	38	22	-	1	-	-	-	-	23
Jones, GA	36+3	-	2	1	-	-	-	39+3	14	-	1	-	-	-	-	15
Jones, H	247	-	14	-	-	1	-	262	-	-	-	-	-	-	-	-
Jones, R	242	-	15	15	-	-	-	272	-	-	-	-	-	-	-	-
Jones, RT	11	-	1	-	-	-	-	12	-	-	-	-	-	-	-	-
Jones, RW	49	-	-	3	-	-	-	52	-	-	-	-	-	-	-	-
Joy, WJ	3	-	-	-	-	-	-	3	-	-	-	-	-	-	-	-
Joyce, JW	14	-	-	-	-	-	-	14	-	-	-	-	-	-	-	-
Joyce, W	119+1	-	9	6	-	-	-	134+1	4	-	-	-	-	-	-	4
Keating, AE	17	-	-	-	-	-	-	17	5	-	-	-	-	-	-	5
Keeley, GM	365+5	-	19+1	23	5	-	-	412+6	23	-	-	-	1	-	-	24
Kelly, AT	10	-	2	2	-	-	-	14	-	-	-	-	-	-	-	-
Kelly, M	3	-	-	-	-	-	-	3	-	-	-	-	-	-	-	-

	APPEARANCES								GOALS							
	LEAGUE	FOOTBALL LEAGUE PLAY-OFFS/ TEST MATCHES	FA CUP	FOOTBALL LEAGUE CUP	FULL MEMBERS' CUP	FA CHARITY SHIELD	EUROPEAN CHAMPIONS LEAGUE, UEFA CUP	TOTAL	LEAGUE	FOOTBALL LEAGUE PLAY-OFFS/ TEST MATCHES	FA CUP	FOOTBALL LEAGUE CUP	FULL MEMBERS' CUP	FA CHARITY SHIELD	EUROPEAN CHAMPIONS LEAGUE, UEFA CUP	TOTAL
Kelly, WM	186	-	16	-	-	-	-	202	1	-	-	-	-	-	-	1
Kendall, H	79	-	6	7	-	-	-	92	6	-	-	1	-	-	-	7
Kenna, JJ	147+1	-	12	14	-	1	6	180+1	1	-	-	-	-	-	-	1
Kennedy, AJ	49+10	1+1	3	4	3	-	-	60+11	23	1	1	-	2	-	-	27
Kennedy, F	29	-	-	-	-	-	-	29	8	-	-	-	-	-	-	8
Kennedy, PA	3	-	-	-	-	-	-	3	-	-	-	-	-	-	-	-
Kenyon, JF	32+14	-	-	-	-	-	-	32+14	7	-	-	-	-	-	-	7
Kerr, J	16	-	-	-	-	-	-	16	-	-	-	-	-	-	-	-
Kerr, JP	11	-	-	-	-	-	-	11	-	-	-	-	-	-	-	-
Killean, E	88	3	6	-	-	-	-	97	6	-	-	-	-	-	-	6
Knighton, K	70	-	2	4	-	-	-	76	11	-	-	1	-	-	-	12
Knowles, A	31	-	4	-	-	-	-	35	-	-	-	-	-	-	-	-
Konde, O	-	-	+1	-	-	-	-	+1	-	-	-	-	-	-	-	-
Kopel, F	23+2	-	-	-	-	-	-	23+2	-	-	-	-	-	-	-	-
Kyle, A	36	-	2	-	-	-	-	38	8	-	-	-	-	-	-	8
Lanceley, E	52	-	2	-	-	-	-	54	-	-	-	-	-	-	-	-
Langton, R	212	-	18	-	-	-	-	230	57	-	1	-	-	-	-	58
Lapham, EH	2	-	-	-	-	-	-	2	-	-	-	-	-	-	-	-
Latham, WH	-	-	2	-	-	-	-	2	-	-	-	-	-	-	-	-
Latheron, EG	256	-	24	-	-	1	-	281	94	-	10	-	-	-	-	104
Law, J	3	-	-	-	-	-	-	3	1	-	-	-	-	-	-	1
Lawrie, J	2	-	-	-	-	-	-	2	-	-	-	-	-	-	-	-
Lawther, WI	59	-	5	11	-	-	-	75	21	-	1	10	-	-	-	32
Leaver, D	14	-	-	-	-	-	-	14	5	-	-	-	-	-	-	5
Leaver, W	-	-	1	-	-	-	-	1	-	-	-	-	-	-	-	-
Lee, JB	-	-	1	-	-	-	-	1	-	-	-	-	-	-	-	-
Lee, WR	1	-	-	-	-	-	-	1	-	-	-	-	-	-	-	-
LeSaux, GP	127+2	-	8	10	-	2	4+1	151+3	7	-	-	-	-	-	-	7
Lewis, FJ	24+4	-	-	2	-	-	-	26+4	6	-	-	-	-	-	-	6
Lewis, J	-	-	3	-	-	-	-	3	-	-	1	-	-	-	-	1
Leyland, HK	166	-	18	4	-	-	-	188	-	-	-	-	-	-	-	-
Livingstone, S	25+5	-	1	2	-	-	-	28+5	10	-	1	-	-	-	-	11
Lofthouse, JM	51	-	32	-	-	-	-	83	18	-	12	-	-	-	-	30
Logan, N	22	-	-	-	-	-	-	22	2	-	-	-	-	-	-	2
Longmuir, AM	24	-	5	-	-	-	-	29	2	-	-	-	-	-	-	2
Lord, F	10	-	-	-	-	-	-	10	1	-	-	-	-	-	-	1
Low, D	13	-	-	-	-	-	-	13	-	-	-	-	-	-	-	-
Lowe, J	2	-	-	-	-	-	-	2	-	-	-	-	-	-	-	-
Lowey, JA	136+5	-	6	9	-	-	-	151+5	14	-	1	1	-	-	-	16
Luke, C	10	-	-	-	-	-	-	10	2	-	-	-	-	-	-	2
McAllister, T	2	-	-	-	-	-	-	2	-	-	-	-	-	-	-	-
McAteer, JW	22+3	-	2	-	-	-	-	24+3	2	-	-	-	-	-	-	2
McCaig, RAM	30	-	2	-	-	-	-	32	2	-	-	-	-	-	-	2
McCall, W	11	-	-	-	-	-	-	11	-	-	-	-	-	-	-	-
McCallum, N	2	-	-	-	-	-	-	2	-	-	-	-	-	-	-	-
McCleery, W	23	-	2	-	-	-	-	25	5	-	-	-	-	-	-	5
McClelland, C	13	-	5	-	-	-	-	18	2	-	5	-	-	-	-	7

	APPEARANCES								GOALS							
	LEAGUE	FOOTBALL LEAGUE PLAY-OFFS/ TEST MATCHES	FA CUP	FOOTBALL LEAGUE CUP	FULL MEMBERS' CUP	FA CHARITY SHIELD	EUROPEAN CHAMPIONS LEAGUE, UEFA CUP	TOTAL	LEAGUE	FOOTBALL LEAGUE PLAY-OFFS/ TEST MATCHES	FA CUP	FOOTBALL LEAGUE CUP	FULL MEMBERS' CUP	FA CHARITY SHIELD	EUROPEAN CHAMPIONS LEAGUE, UEFA CUP	TOTAL
McClure, S	144	-	8	-	-	-	-	152	12	-	-	-	-	-	-	12
McCulloch, SS	1	-	-	-	-	-	-	1	-	-	-	-	-	-	-	-
McDonald, G	19+2	-	+2	3	-	-	-	22+4	2	-	-	-	-	-	-	2
McDonald, John	1	-	-	-	-	-	-	1	-	-	-	-	-	-	-	-
McDonald, John	33	-	2	-	-	-	-	35	7	-	-	-	-	-	-	7
McEvoy, MA	183	-	17	13	-	-	-	213	89	-	10	4	-	-	-	103
MacFarlane, R	2	-	-	-	-	-	-	2	-	-	-	-	-	-	-	-
McGhie, A	23	-	2	-	-	-	-	25	3	-	-	-	-	-	-	3
McGorrighan, FO	5	-	-	-	-	-	-	5	-	-	-	-	-	-	-	-
McGrath, M	268	-	29	15	-	-	-	312	8	-	3	1	-	-	-	12
McGrogan, F	4	-	-	-	-	-	-	4	1	-	-	-	-	-	-	1
McIntyre, H	-	-	34	-	-	-	-	34	-	-	4	-	-	-	-	4
McIntyre, JM	175	-	19	-	-	-	-	194	38	-	-	-	-	-	-	38
McIver, W	126	-	6	-	-	-	-	132	-	-	-	-	-	-	-	-
McKay, J	150	-	11	-	-	-	-	161	46	-	3	-	-	-	-	49
McKee, WA	1	-	-	-	-	-	-	1	-	-	-	-	-	-	-	-
McKenzie, D	74	-	8	8	-	-	-	90	16	-	1	4	-	-	-	21
McKeown, TM	19	-	2	-	-	-	-	21	-	-	-	-	-	-	-	-
McKinlay, WJA	76+14	-	7+1	4	-	-	1	88+15	3	-	-	1	-	-	-	4
McKinnell, JTB	111	-	13	-	-	-	-	124	-	-	-	-	-	-	-	-
McKinnon, P	5	-	1	-	1	-	-	7	-	-	-	-	-	-	-	-
McLean, JC	8	-	-	-	-	-	-	8	-	-	-	-	-	-	-	-
McLean, T	247	-	27	-	-	1	-	275	44	-	5	-	-	-	-	49
McLean, W	12	-	2	-	-	-	-	14	-	-	-	-	-	-	-	-
MacLeod, AR	193	-	23	2	-	-	-	218	47	-	6	-	-	-	-	53
McLuckie, GR	20	-	1	-	-	-	-	21	2	-	1	-	-	-	-	3
McNamee, J	56	-	1	-	-	-	-	57	9	-	1	-	-	-	-	10
McOwen, WA	14	-	1	-	-	-	-	15	-	-	-	-	-	-	-	-
McShane, H	2	-	-	-	-	-	-	2	-	-	-	-	-	-	-	-
Mail, D	200+6	8	12	12+1	9	-	-	241+7	4	-	-	-	-	-	-	4
Makel, LR	1+5	-	-	+3	-	+1	1+2	2+11	-	-	-	-	-	-	-	-
Malcolm, W	2	-	-	-	-	-	-	2	-	-	-	-	-	-	-	-
Mann, GW	2	-	-	-	-	-	-	2	1	-	-	-	-	-	-	1
Manning, JT	4	-	-	-	-	-	-	4	-	-	-	-	-	-	-	-
Manson, R	16	-	-	-	-	-	-	16	3	-	-	-	-	-	-	3
Marcolin, D	5+5	-	3	2	-	-	-	10+5	1	-	-	-	-	-	-	1
Marker, NRT	41+13	-	4+1	3+1	-	+1	1	49+16	1	-	-	-	-	-	-	1
Marks, WG	67	-	7	-	-	-	-	74	-	-	-	-	-	-	-	-
Marriott, A	2	-	-	-	-	-	-	2	-	-	-	-	-	-	-	-
Marshall, H	53	4	9	-	-	-	-	66	2	-	-	-	-	-	-	2
Martin, D	218+6	-	10+1	16+1	-	-	-	244+8	57	-	2	4	-	-	-	63
Martin, J	57	-	5	-	-	-	-	62	25	-	2	-	-	-	-	27
Matier, G	20	-	1	-	-	-	-	21	-	-	-	-	-	-	-	-
May, D	123	3	10	12+1	2	-	-	150+1	3	-	1	2	-	-	-	6
Melville, J	25	-	-	-	-	-	-	25	-	-	-	-	-	-	-	-
Metcalfe, SM	376+11	-	23	22+2	-	-	-	421+13	21	-	1	3	-	-	-	25
Millar, J	122+4	8	4	9+1	2	-	-	145+5	1	-	-	-	-	-	-	1
Miller, AB	6	-	-	-	-	-	-	6	-	-	-	-	-	-	-	-
Miller, I	252+16	4	12+1	10+2	5+3	-	-	283+22	16	-	-	1	1	-	-	18

	APPEARANCES								GOALS							
	LEAGUE	FOOTBALL LEAGUE PLAY-OFFS/ TEST MATCHES	FA CUP	FOOTBALL LEAGUE CUP	FULL MEMBERS' CUP	FA CHARITY SHIELD	EUROPEAN CHAMPIONS LEAGUE, UEFA CUP	TOTAL	LEAGUE	FOOTBALL LEAGUE PLAY-OFFS/ TEST MATCHES	FA CUP	FOOTBALL LEAGUE CUP	FULL MEMBERS' CUP	FA CHARITY SHIELD	EUROPEAN CHAMPIONS LEAGUE, UEFA CUP	TOTAL
Mills, A	2	1	-	-	-	-	-	3	-	-	-	-	-	-	-	-
Milne, JV	45	-	4	-	-	-	-	49	13	-	2	-	-	-	-	15
Mimms, RA	132+2	3	9	15	1	-	-	160+2	-	-	-	-	-	-	-	-
Mitchell, AJ	3	-	-	-	-	-	-	3	-	-	-	-	-	-	-	-
Mitchell, R	17+12	-	2	-	-	-	-	19+12	6	-	1	-	-	-	-	7
Mitchell, T	73	-	9	-	-	-	-	82	27	-	4	-	-	-	-	31
Mitchell, W	1	-	-	-	-	-	-	1	2	-	-	-	-	-	-	2
Moir, J	77	-	3	-	-	-	-	80	-	-	-	-	-	-	-	-
Monks, A	24	-	3	-	-	-	-	27	4	-	1	-	-	-	-	5
Mooney, F	58	-	1	-	-	-	-	59	19	-	-	-	-	-	-	19
Moore, NW	7	-	-	-	-	-	-	7	1	-	-	-	-	-	-	1
Moran, KB	143+4	5	10+1	8+1	1	-	-	167+6	10	1	1	-	-	-	-	12
Moreland, J	20	1	-	-	-	-	-	21	6	-	-	-	-	-	-	6
Morgan, H	77	-	2	-	-	-	-	79	18	-	-	-	-	-	-	18
Morley, BJ	20	-	-	4	-	-	-	24	-	-	-	-	-	-	-	-
Morris, PA	2+2	-	1+1	-	-	-	-	3+3	-	-	-	-	-	-	-	-
Morrison, AC	1+4	-	1	-	-	-	-	2+4	-	-	-	-	-	-	-	-
Mortimer, R	16	-	-	-	-	-	-	16	4	-	-	-	-	-	-	4
Mullen, J	6+4	-	2	-	-	-	-	8+4	-	-	-	-	-	-	-	-
Mulvaney, R	135+6	-	2	8	-	-	-	145+6	4	-	-	-	-	-	-	4
Munro, S	1	-	-	-	-	-	-	1	-	-	-	-	-	-	-	-
Murphy, DP	1+2	-	-	-	-	-	-	1+2	-	-	-	-	-	-	-	-
Murphy, TE	31	-	3	-	-	-	-	34	6	-	1	-	-	-	-	7
Murray, JW	109	-	13	-	-	-	-	122	-	-	-	-	-	-	-	-
Murray, RW	10	-	-	-	-	-	-	10	-	-	-	-	-	-	-	-
Napier, CRA	53+1	-	7	3	-	-	-	63+1	10	-	3	-	-	-	-	13
Needham, PA	4+1	-	-	1+1	-	-	-	5+2	-	-	-	-	-	-	-	-
Newell, MC	113+17	3	9+2	14+2	-	1	5+1	145+22	28	2	6	8	-	-	4	48
Newton, KR	306	-	21	30	-	-	-	357	9	-	-	1	-	-	-	10
Nicol, T	16	-	3	-	-	-	-	19	2	-	-	-	-	-	-	2
Nightingale, A	35	-	7	-	-	-	-	42	5	-	3	-	-	-	-	8
Oakes, J	35	-	2	-	-	-	-	37	9	-	-	-	-	-	-	9
Oates, G	76	-	4	6	-	-	-	86	10	-	1	-	-	-	-	11
O'Brien, J	3	-	-	-	-	-	-	3	-	-	-	-	-	-	-	-
O'Dowd, JP	50	-	-	-	-	1	-	51	-	-	-	-	-	-	-	-
Ogilvie, A	108	-	12	-	-	-	-	120	-	-	-	-	-	-	-	-
O'Keefe, JV	68	-	1	7	6	-	-	82	-	-	-	-	-	-	-	-
Oldham, W	9	-	-	-	-	-	-	9	1	-	-	-	-	-	-	1
O'Leary, DP	6	-	1	-	-	-	-	7	1	-	-	-	-	-	-	1
Oliver, A	2	-	-	-	-	-	-	2	-	-	-	-	-	-	-	-
Oliver, N	5+1	-	-	1+1	1	-	-	7+2	-	-	-	-	-	-	-	-
O'Mara, J	30+5	-	5+1	1	-	-	-	36+6	10	-	2	-	-	-	-	12
Orr, J	75	-	10	-	-	-	-	85	30	-	3	-	-	-	-	33
Ostenstad, E	12+4	-	+1	1	-	-	-	13+5	6	-	-	-	-	-	-	6
Parker, H	3	-	-	-	-	-	-	3	-	-	-	-	-	-	-	-
Parker, SJ	5+4	-	-	1	-	-	-	6+4	1	-	-	-	-	-	-	1
Parkes, A	345+5	-	21	21	-	-	-	387+5	38	-	4	3	-	-	-	45

	APPEARANCES								GOALS							
	LEAGUE	FOOTBALL LEAGUE PLAY-OFFS/ TEST MATCHES	FA CUP	FOOTBALL LEAGUE CUP	FULL MEMBERS' CUP	FA CHARITY SHIELD	EUROPEAN CHAMPIONS LEAGUE, UEFA CUP	TOTAL	LEAGUE	FOOTBALL LEAGUE PLAY-OFFS/ TEST MATCHES	FA CUP	FOOTBALL LEAGUE CUP	FULL MEMBERS' CUP	FA CHARITY SHIELD	EUROPEAN CHAMPIONS LEAGUE, UEFA CUP	TOTAL
Parkin, TJ	13	-	-	-	-	-	-	13	-	-	-	-	-	-	-	-
Parkinson, J	1	-	-	-	-	-	-	1	-	-	-	-	-	-	-	-
Patterson, JG	107	-	5	-	-	-	-	112	-	-	-	-	-	-	-	-
Patterson, MA	89+12	-	3+1	4	2+4	-	-	98+17	20	-	-	1	1	-	-	22
Paul, AG	1	-	1	-	-	-	-	2	-	-	-	-	-	-	-	-
Peacock, D	36+4	-	4	4	-	-	2	46+4	1	-	-	-	-	-	-	1
Pearce, IA	43+19	-	1+2	4+4	-	2	4+1	54+26	2	-	-	1	-	-	-	3
Pearce, RG	1	-	-	-	-	-	-	1	-	-	-	-	-	-	-	-
Pedersen, PW	6+5	-	-	1+1	-	-	-	7+6	1	-	-	-	-	-	-	1
Pedersen, T	3+2	-	-	3	-	-	-	6+2	-	-	-	-	-	-	-	-
Pennington, R	8	-	2	-	-	-	-	10	-	-	-	-	-	-	-	-
Pentland, FB	51	-	1	-	-	-	-	52	9	-	-	-	-	-	-	9
Perez, S	4+1	-	1	-	-	-	2	7+1	1	-	-	-	-	-	1	2
Pickering, F	134	-	10	14	-	-	-	158	61	-	5	8	-	-	-	74
Pinkerton, JR	1	-	-	-	-	-	-	1	-	-	-	-	-	-	-	-
Pinxton, AE	3	-	1	-	-	-	-	4	-	-	-	-	-	-	-	-
Platt, P	1	-	-	-	-	-	-	1	-	-	-	-	-	-	-	-
Pool, A	17	-	2	-	-	-	-	19	-	-	-	-	-	-	-	-
Porteous, G	6	-	-	-	-	-	-	6	-	-	-	-	-	-	-	-
Porter, R	1	-	-	-	-	-	-	1	-	-	-	-	-	-	-	-
Porter, WS	6	-	-	-	-	-	-	6	-	-	-	-	-	-	-	-
Pratt, JT	6	-	2	-	-	-	-	8	-	-	-	-	-	-	-	-
Price, CJ	96+6	3	2	7	6	-	-	114+6	14	-	-	-	-	-	-	14
Price, J	63+13	-	4+2	1+1	-	-	-	68+16	12	-	-	-	-	-	-	12
Priday, RH	44	-	1	-	-	-	-	45	11	-	-	-	-	-	-	11
Proctor, BJ	2	-	1	-	-	-	-	3	-	-	-	-	-	-	-	-
Proudfoot, J	36	1	1	-	-	-	-	38	14	-	-	-	-	-	-	14
Pryde, RI	320	-	25	-	-	-	-	345	11	-	-	-	-	-	-	11
Puddefoot, SC	250	-	26	-	-	1	-	277	79	-	8	-	-	-	-	87
Quigley, E	159	-	7	-	-	-	-	166	92	-	3	-	-	-	-	95
Quinn, D	1	-	-	-	-	-	-	1	-	-	-	-	-	-	-	-
Quinn, JM	58+13	-	4	6+1	2	-	-	70+14	17	-	3	2	1	-	-	23
Radford, J	36	-	1	1	-	-	-	38	10	-	1	-	-	-	-	11
Raitt, D	4	-	-	-	-	-	-	4	-	-	-	-	-	-	-	-
Ralphs, BVH	40	-	1	-	-	-	-	41	6	-	-	-	-	-	-	6
Ramsbottom, N	10	-	-	-	-	-	-	10	-	-	-	-	-	-	-	-
Randell, CW	72+1	-	5	4	-	-	-	81+1	7	-	-	-	-	-	-	7
Rankin, W	144	-	18	-	-	-	-	162	4	-	-	-	-	-	-	4
Ratcliffe, JB	36	-	5	9	-	-	-	50	4	-	1	3	-	-	-	8
Rathbone, MJ	270+3	-	15	14	4	-	-	303+3	2	-	-	-	-	-	-	2
Reeves, TB	12	-	5	-	-	-	-	17	-	-	-	-	-	-	-	-
Reid, NS	160+14	8	6+2	13	5+1	-	-	192+17	9	-	-	-	1	-	-	10
Reilly, F	127	-	11	-	-	-	-	138	8	-	1	-	-	-	-	9
Reitmaier, K	-	-	-	-	1	-	-	1	-	-	-	-	-	-	-	-
Richards, JW	2	-	-	-	-	-	-	2	-	-	-	-	-	-	-	-
Richardson, LJ	50+12	1+2	-	1+2	1	-	-	53+16	3	-	-	-	-	-	-	3
Richardson, LN	-	-	-	1	-	-	-	1	-	-	-	-	-	-	-	-

	APPEARANCES								GOALS							
	LEAGUE	FOOTBALL LEAGUE PLAY-OFFS/ TEST MATCHES	FA CUP	FOOTBALL LEAGUE CUP	FULL MEMBERS' CUP	FA CHARITY SHIELD	EUROPEAN CHAMPIONS LEAGUE, UEFA CUP	TOTAL	LEAGUE	FOOTBALL LEAGUE PLAY-OFFS/ TEST MATCHES	FA CUP	FOOTBALL LEAGUE CUP	FULL MEMBERS' CUP	FA CHARITY SHIELD	EUROPEAN CHAMPIONS LEAGUE, UEFA CUP	TOTAL
Rigby, A	156	-	12	-	-	1	-	169	41	-	3	-	-	-	-	44
Rigg, T	12	-	-	-	-	-	-	12	-	-	-	-	-	-	-	-
Riley, T	22	-	2	-	-	-	-	24	-	-	-	-	-	-	-	-
Ripley, SE	172+15	-	14	18	-	2	6+1	212+16	13	-	3	-	-	-	-	16
Ritchie, GT	2	-	-	-	-	-	-	2	-	-	-	-	-	-	-	-
Roberts, JT	3	-	-	-	-	-	-	3	-	-	-	-	-	-	-	-
Roberts, T	6	-	-	-	-	-	-	6	-	-	-	-	-	-	-	-
Robertson, G	10	-	3	-	-	-	-	13	1	-	-	-	-	-	-	1
Robertson, J	78	-	7	-	-	-	-	85	22	-	-	-	-	-	-	22
Robinson, A	144	-	12	-	-	1	-	157	-	-	-	-	-	-	-	-
Robinson, P	18	-	-	-	-	-	-	18	2	-	-	-	-	-	-	2
Rodgers, N	43	-	5	-	-	-	-	48	21	-	3	-	-	-	-	24
Rogers, E	159+6	-	4	14	-	-	-	177+6	30	-	-	9	-	-	-	39
Rogers, W	73	-	10	-	-	-	-	83	24	-	3	-	-	-	-	27
Rollo, D	207	-	18	-	-	-	-	225	5	-	1	-	-	-	-	6
Roscamp, J	223	-	26	-	-	1	-	250	37	-	7	-	-	-	-	44
Rostron, T	-	-	1	-	-	-	-	1	-	-	1	-	-	-	-	1
Round, P	41+10	-	4	5	-	-	-	50+10	5	-	-	-	-	-	-	5
Roxburgh, R	114	-	13	-	-	1	-	128	-	-	-	-	-	-	-	-
Rushton, W	-	-	4	-	-	-	-	4	-	-	1	-	-	-	-	1
Russell, A	22+2	-	1	1	-	-	-	24+2	4	-	-	-	-	-	-	4
Russell, J	1	-	-	-	-	-	-	1	-	-	-	-	-	-	-	-
Rutherford, S	13	-	1	-	-	-	-	14	1	-	-	-	-	-	-	1
Sale, T	65	-	3	-	-	-	-	68	25	-	1	-	-	-	-	26
Salmon, MB	1	-	-	-	-	-	-	1	-	-	-	-	-	-	-	-
Sanderson, GA	4	-	1	-	-	-	-	5	-	-	-	-	-	-	-	-
Sandham, W	4	-	-	-	-	-	-	4	1	-	-	-	-	-	-	1
Sawers, W	24	-	4	-	-	-	-	28	11	-	3	-	-	-	-	14
Sellars, S	194+8	11	11	12	9	-	-	237+8	35	2	1	3	-	-	-	41
Sewell, WR	227	-	21	-	-	-	-	248	-	-	-	-	-	-	-	-
Shanahan, TC	6	-	-	-	-	-	-	6	2	-	-	-	-	-	-	2
Sharp, A	9	-	-	-	-	-	-	9	1	-	-	-	-	-	-	1
Sharples, GFV	99+4	-	5	4+1	-	-	-	108+5	5	-	-	-	-	-	-	5
Sharples, H	-	-	4	-	-	-	-	4	-	-	1	-	-	-	-	1
Shaw, GR	5	-	-	-	-	-	-	5	2	-	-	-	-	-	-	2
Shea, D	97	-	8	-	-	-	-	105	62	-	3	-	-	-	-	65
Shearer, A	132+6	-	8	16	-	1	8	165+6	112	-	2	14	-	-	2	130
Shearer, DN	5+1	+1	-	-	-	-	-	5+2	1	-	-	-	-	-	-	1
Shepstone, PTA	16+10	-	+1	1	1	-	-	18+11	1	-	-	-	-	-	-	1
Sherrington, J	1	-	-	-	-	-	-	1	-	-	-	-	-	-	-	-
Sherwood, TA	239+7	-	15+2	24+1	-	2	10	290+10	26	-	4	2	-	-	-	32
Shorrock, F	-	-	1	-	-	-	-	1	-	-	-	-	-	-	-	-
Short, CJ	10	-	-	1	-	-	-	11	-	-	-	-	-	-	-	-
Silvester, PD	5	-	-	-	-	-	-	5	1	-	-	-	-	-	-	1
Simpson, J	151	-	17	-	-	1	-	169	15	-	7	-	-	-	-	22
Simpson, WS	4	-	-	-	-	-	-	4	-	-	-	-	-	-	-	-
Sims, HC	13	-	-	-	-	-	-	13	-	-	-	-	-	-	-	-
Skinner, CR	11+5	-	1	+1	3	-	-	15+6	-	-	-	-	1	-	-	1

	APPEARANCES								GOALS							
	LEAGUE	FOOTBALL LEAGUE PLAY-OFFS/ TEST MATCHES	FA CUP	FOOTBALL LEAGUE CUP	FULL MEMBERS' CUP	FA CHARITY SHIELD	EUROPEAN CHAMPIONS LEAGUE, UEFA CUP	TOTAL	LEAGUE	FOOTBALL LEAGUE PLAY-OFFS/ TEST MATCHES	FA CUP	FOOTBALL LEAGUE CUP	FULL MEMBERS' CUP	FA CHARITY SHIELD	EUROPEAN CHAMPIONS LEAGUE, UEFA CUP	TOTAL
Slater, RD	12+6	-	1	1	-	1	1	16+6	-	-	-	-	-	-	-	-
Smailes, M	4	-	-	-	-	-	-	4	-	-	-	-	-	-	-	-
Smeaton, JR	38	-	-	-	-	-	-	38	9	-	-	-	-	-	-	9
Smethams, JC	3	-	-	-	-	-	-	3	-	-	-	-	-	-	-	-
Smith, A	7	-	-	-	-	-	-	7	-	-	-	-	-	-	-	-
Smith, G	58	-	3	-	-	-	-	61	4	-	-	-	-	-	-	4
Smith, J	30	-	4	-	-	-	-	34	12	-	-	-	-	-	-	12
Smith, PJ	172	-	20	-	-	1	-	193	5	-	1	-	-	-	-	6
Smith, WA	1	-	-	-	-	-	-	1	-	-	-	-	-	-	-	-
Smith, WH	119	-	9	-	-	-	-	128	10	-	2	-	-	-	-	12
Somers, P	76	-	2	-	-	-	-	78	13	-	-	-	-	-	-	13
Sorley, J	26	-	1	-	-	-	-	27	9	-	-	-	-	-	-	9
Southworth, James	21	-	6	-	-	-	-	27	-	-	-	-	-	-	-	-
Southworth, John	108	-	24	-	-	-	-	132	97	-	24	-	-	-	-	121
Sowerbutts, JE	-	-	20	-	-	-	-	20	-	-	16	-	-	-	-	16
Speedie, DR	34+2	3	2	2	-	-	-	41+2	23	2	1	-	-	-	-	26
Speight, M	50+1	-	-	6	-	-	-	56+1	4	-	-	-	-	-	-	4
Stapleton, FA	80+1	2	4	5	1	-	-	92+1	13	-	1	1	-	-	-	15
Starbuck, PM	5+1	-	-	-	-	-	-	5+1	1	-	-	-	-	-	-	1
Stephan, HW	13	-	2	-	-	-	-	15	1	-	-	-	-	-	-	1
Stephenson, RA	21	-	6	-	-	-	-	27	5	-	-	-	-	-	-	5
Stevenson, H	58	-	4	-	-	-	-	62	3	-	-	-	-	-	-	3
Stonehouse, K	77+8	-	2	3+1	-	-	-	82+9	27	-	-	2	-	-	-	29
Stothert, J	1	-	-	-	-	-	-	1	1	-	-	-	-	-	-	1
Strachan, T	-	-	21	-	-	-	-	21	-	-	6	-	-	-	-	6
Stringfellow, J	4	-	-	-	-	-	-	4	-	-	-	-	-	-	-	-
Stuart, J	15	-	-	-	-	-	-	15	5	-	-	-	-	-	-	5
Suart, R	176	-	11	-	-	-	-	187	-	-	-	-	-	-	-	-
Sulley, CS	134	5	6	6	5	-	-	156	3	-	-	-	-	-	-	3
Suter, F	1	-	38	-	-	-	-	39	-	-	3	-	-	-	-	3
Suttie, T	103	-	7	-	-	-	-	110	-	-	-	-	-	-	-	-
Sutton, CR	125+5	-	9	11+1	-	1	6+3	152+9	47	-	4	7	-	-	1	59
Svarc, RL	42+8	-	4	3+1	-	-	-	49+9	16	-	1	3	-	-	-	20
Swarbrick, J	15	-	1	-	-	-	-	16	-	-	-	-	-	-	-	-
Swift, ES	2	-	-	-	-	-	-	2	-	-	-	-	-	-	-	-
Swindells, J	9	-	-	-	-	-	-	9	1	-	-	-	-	-	-	1
Talbot, FL	90	-	6	-	-	-	-	96	20	-	1	-	-	-	-	21
Taylor, G	62+2	-	2+1	2	-	-	-	66+3	3	-	-	-	-	-	-	3
Taylor, KG	200	-	22	11	-	-	-	233	-	-	-	-	-	-	-	-
Taylor, M	5+4	-	1	2	-	-	+1	8+5	-	-	-	-	-	-	-	-
Taylor, R	3	-	-	-	-	-	-	3	1	-	-	-	-	-	-	1
Taylor, W	10	-	3	-	-	-	-	13	1	-	1	-	-	-	-	2
Thomas, E	37	-	2	5	-	-	-	44	9	-	1	5	-	-	-	15
Thompson, CD	81+4	-	10	5	-	-	-	96+4	24	-	2	-	-	-	-	26
Thompson, JE	171	-	8	-	-	-	-	179	82	-	2	-	-	-	-	84
Thompson, R	9	-	-	-	-	-	-	9	-	-	-	-	-	-	-	-
Thorley, D	2+2	-	-	-	-	-	-	2+2	-	-	-	-	-	-	-	-
Thorne, PL	-	-	-	-	-	+1	-	+1	-	-	-	-	-	-	-	-
Thornewell, G	41	-	6	-	-	1	-	48	4	-	1	-	-	1	-	6

	APPEARANCES								GOALS							
	LEAGUE	FOOTBALL LEAGUE PLAY-OFFS/ TEST MATCHES	FA CUP	FOOTBALL LEAGUE CUP	FULL MEMBERS' CUP	FA CHARITY SHIELD	EUROPEAN CHAMPIONS LEAGUE, UEFA CUP	TOTAL	LEAGUE	FOOTBALL LEAGUE PLAY-OFFS/ TEST MATCHES	FA CUP	FOOTBALL LEAGUE CUP	FULL MEMBERS' CUP	FA CHARITY SHIELD	EUROPEAN CHAMPIONS LEAGUE, UEFA CUP	TOTAL
Thorpe, L	85	-	7	-	-	-	-	92	1	-	-	-	-	-	-	1
Tierney, TT	21	-	-	-	-	-	-	21	3	-	-	-	-	-	-	3
Todd, PR	46	-	1	-	-	-	-	47	13	-	-	-	-	-	-	13
Tomlinson, J	1	-	-	-	-	-	-	1	-	-	-	-	-	-	-	-
Tomlinson, RW	25	-	4	-	-	-	-	29	-	-	-	-	-	-	-	-
Townley, WJ	97	-	26	-	-	-	-	123	37	-	14	-	-	-	-	51
Turnbull, P	26	-	1	-	-	-	-	27	7	-	1	-	-	-	-	8
Turner, DJ	23+2	-	1	-	-	-	-	24+2	-	-	-	-	-	-	-	-
Turner, RG	-	-	9	-	-	-	-	9	-	-	-	-	-	-	-	-
Turner, TS	113	-	2	-	-	-	-	115	24	-	-	-	-	-	-	24
Tyson, WG	6	-	-	-	-	-	-	6	2	-	-	-	-	-	-	2
Valery, PJC	14+1	-	1+1	2	-	-	-	17+2	-	-	-	-	-	-	-	-
Vause, PG	7	-	1	-	-	-	-	8	1	-	-	-	-	-	-	1
Venters, A	25	-	-	-	-	-	-	25	7	-	-	-	-	-	-	7
Vernon, TR	131	-	13	-	-	-	-	144	49	-	3	-	-	-	-	52
Waddington, J	139+9	-	12	7+1	-	-	-	158+10	18	-	2	-	-	-	-	20
Wade, JJ	1	-	-	-	-	-	-	1	2	-	-	-	-	-	-	2
Wagstaffe, D	74+3	-	4	4	-	-	-	82+3	7	-	-	-	-	-	-	7
Walmsley, A	272	-	28	-	-	1	-	301	6	-	-	-	-	-	-	6
Walmsley, R	38	-	1	-	-	-	-	39	-	-	-	-	-	-	-	-
Walter, JD	27	-	-	-	-	-	-	27	2	-	-	-	-	-	-	2
Walton, N	110	-	29	-	-	-	-	139	37	-	12	-	-	-	-	49
Walton, WE	5	-	-	-	-	-	-	5	1	-	-	-	-	-	-	1
Ward, AS	36+1	-	4+1	2	-	-	-	42+2	11	-	-	-	-	-	-	11
Ward, JT	-	-	2	-	-	-	-	2	-	-	-	-	-	-	-	-
Warhurst, P	30+27	-	2+1	6+2	-	-	4+2	42+32	4	-	-	-	-	-	-	4
Waring, C	1	-	-	-	-	-	-	1	-	-	-	-	-	-	-	-
Waring, W	1	-	-	-	-	-	-	1	-	-	-	-	-	-	-	-
Watson, JW	12	-	-	-	-	-	-	12	-	-	-	-	-	-	-	-
Watson, LP	55	-	6	-	-	-	-	61	19	-	1	-	-	-	-	20
Watts, C	9	-	-	-	-	-	-	9	-	-	-	-	-	-	-	-
Webber, JV	8	-	-	-	-	-	-	8	1	-	-	-	-	-	-	1
Webster, MV	2	-	-	-	-	-	-	2	-	-	-	-	-	-	-	-
Weddle, JR	42	-	7	-	-	-	-	49	16	-	2	-	-	-	-	18
Wegerle, RC	20+14	-	4+1	3+3	-	-	-	27+18	6	-	2	4	-	-	-	12
Weir, JB	23	-	-	-	-	-	-	23	7	-	-	-	-	-	-	7
Westby, JL	2	-	-	-	-	-	-	2	-	-	-	-	-	-	-	-
Westcott, D	63	-	3	-	-	-	-	66	37	-	-	-	-	-	-	37
Whalley, JH	2	-	-	1	-	-	-	3	-	-	-	-	-	-	-	-
Wharton, JE	129	-	9	-	-	-	-	138	15	-	2	-	-	-	-	17
Wheeler, AJ	21	-	-	-	-	-	-	21	5	-	-	-	-	-	-	5
Whelan, D	78	-	9	-	-	-	-	87	3	-	-	-	-	-	-	3
Whitehead, J	85	-	8	-	-	-	-	93	22	-	2	-	-	-	-	24
Whitehead, W	3	-	1	-	-	-	-	4	1	-	-	-	-	-	-	1
Whiteside, A	218	-	21	-	-	-	-	239	3	-	-	-	-	-	-	3
Whittaker, A	250	-	15	-	-	-	-	265	57	-	-	-	-	-	-	57
Whittaker, J	4	-	-	-	-	-	-	4	1	-	-	-	-	-	-	1
Whittaker, W	52	-	1	-	-	-	-	53	-	-	-	-	-	-	-	-

	APPEARANCES								GOALS							
	LEAGUE	FOOTBALL LEAGUE PLAY-OFFS/ TEST MATCHES	FA CUP	FOOTBALL LEAGUE CUP	FULL MEMBERS' CUP	FA CHARITY SHIELD	EUROPEAN CHAMPIONS LEAGUE, UEFA CUP	TOTAL	LEAGUE	FOOTBALL LEAGUE PLAY-OFFS/ TEST MATCHES	FA CUP	FOOTBALL LEAGUE CUP	FULL MEMBERS' CUP	FA CHARITY SHIELD	EUROPEAN CHAMPIONS LEAGUE, UEFA CUP	TOTAL
Whittle, M	5+2	-	-	-	-	-	-	5+2	-	-	-	-	-	-	-	-
Whyte, C	87	-	1	-	-	-	-	88	-	-	-	-	-	-	-	-
Whyte, J	26	-	-	-	-	-	-	26	2	-	-	-	-	-	-	2
Wightman, JR	66	-	5	-	-	-	-	71	2	-	-	-	-	-	-	2
Wilcox, JM	242+27	-	18+2	16+1	2	1	4	283+30	31	-	2	1	-	-	-	34
Wilkie, J	75	2	5	-	-	-	-	82	17	-	1	-	-	-	-	18
Wilkie, T	5	-	-	-	-	-	-	5	-	-	-	-	-	-	-	-
Wilkinson, DL	1	-	-	-	-	-	-	1	-	-	-	-	-	-	-	-
Wilkinson, N	27+3	-	2	5+1	-	-	-	34+4	-	-	-	-	-	-	-	-
Williams, W	31	-	-	-	-	-	-	31	1	-	-	-	-	-	-	1
Williamson, J	9	-	-	-	-	-	-	9	3	-	-	-	-	-	-	3
Williamson, PJ	+1	-	-	-	-	-	-	+1	-	-	-	-	-	-	-	-
Williamson, TR	19	-	-	-	-	-	-	19	1	-	-	-	-	-	-	1
Willis, JJ	1	-	-	-	-	-	-	1	-	-	-	-	-	-	-	-
Wilmington, T	9	-	-	-	-	-	-	9	-	-	-	-	-	-	-	-
Wilson, J	43	-	3	-	-	-	-	46	4	-	-	-	-	-	-	4
Wilson, R	3	-	-	-	-	-	-	3	-	-	-	-	-	-	-	-
Wilson, TC	1	-	-	-	-	-	-	1	-	-	-	-	-	-	-	-
Wilson, W	246+1	-	14	16	-	-	-	276+1	-	-	-	-	-	-	-	-
Witschge, R	1	-	-	-	-	-	-	1	-	-	-	-	-	-	-	-
Wolstenholme, S	98	-	7	-	-	-	-	105	1	-	1	-	-	-	-	2
Wombwell, R	15	-	-	-	-	-	-	15	1	-	-	-	-	-	-	1
Wood, MJ	140+8	-	10+1	6+1	-	-	-	156+10	2	-	-	-	-	-	-	2
Wood, W	7	-	-	-	-	-	-	7	-	-	-	-	-	-	-	-
Woods, M	260	-	30	17	-	-	-	307	2	-	1	-	-	-	-	3
Woolfall, A	-	-	3	-	-	-	-	3	-	-	-	-	-	-	-	-
Woolley, HG	1	-	-	-	-	-	-	1	-	-	-	-	-	-	-	-
Wright, AG	67+7	3	5+1	8	-	-	-	83+8	1	-	-	-	-	-	-	1
Wright, AW	22	-	-	-	-	-	-	22	10	-	-	-	-	-	-	10
Wright, GM	1	-	-	-	-	-	-	1	-	-	-	-	-	-	-	-
Wrigley, BJ	1	-	-	-	-	-	-	1	-	-	-	-	-	-	-	-
Wyles, TC	-	-	2	-	-	-	-	2	-	-	1	-	-	-	-	1
Wylie, T	174	-	17	-	-	-	-	191	-	-	-	-	-	-	-	-
Yarwood, J	1	-	-	-	-	-	-	1	-	-	-	-	-	-	-	-
Young, W	6	-	-	-	-	-	-	6	-	-	-	-	-	-	-	-

Acknowledgements

Written by
PAUL AGNEW

Editor
JIM QUICK*

Art Director
MARK DYSON*

Production Manager
KATH PEARCE*

Production Assistant
KATE WALSH*

Editorial Contributors
KEVIN EMMOTT
MARK BURROW
MATTHEW FIELDING

*DRUMHAWK COMMUNICATIONS

Photography
PAPR
LANCASHIRE EVENING TELEGRAPH
ACTION IMAGES
ROY BEARDSWORTH
(Mike Newell photo)

Special thanks to:
GEOFF AND LYNN HINDLE
DEREK JONES
JOHN HOLDEN
BLACKBURN MUSEUM
BLACKBURN LIBRARY

Published for Blackburn Rovers by
ARROW PUBLISHING
Lytham Assembly Rooms
Dicconson Terrace
Lytham St. Annes
Lancashire
FY8 5JY
Tel: (01253) 731824
Fax: (01253) 731823

Artwork by
TYPEHOUSE
Leyland, Lancashire

Reprographics by
NEUTRON STAR LIMITED
Lytham St. Annes, Lancashire

Printed by
BAHSON COLOUR PRINT LIMITED
Leeds, West Yorkshire.

Finally, we would like to thank everyone who helped during the publication for their time and effort...
...we couldn't have done it without you!

Design & Art Direction,
Drumhawk Communications

ISBN No. 1-900722-16-X